Job Interview

The Ultimate Guide To Crushing Every Interview Question With Confidence And Amazing Body Language To Land Your Dream Job

(Your Guide To Winning In Job Interviews)

John Stapleton

Published by Rob Miles

John Stapleton

All Rights Reserved

Job Interview: The Ultimate Guide To Crushing Every Interview Question With Confidence And Amazing Body Language To Land Your Dream Job (Your Guide To Winning In Job Interviews)

ISBN 978-1-989990-70-4

All rights reserved. No part of this guide may be reproduced in any form without permission in writing from the publisher except in the case of brief quotations embodied in critical articles or reviews.

LEGAL & DISCLAIMER

The information contained in this book is not designed to replace or take the place of any form of medicine or professional medical advice. The information in this book has been provided for educational and entertainment purposes only.

The information contained in this book has been compiled from sources deemed reliable, and it is accurate to the best of the Author's knowledge; however, the Author cannot guarantee its accuracy and validity and cannot be held liable for any errors or omissions. Changes are periodically made to this book. You must consult your doctor or get professional medical advice before using any of the suggested remedies, techniques, or information in this book.

Upon using the information contained in this book, you agree to hold harmless the Author from and against any damages, costs, and expenses, including any legal fees potentially resulting from the application of any of the information provided by this guide. This disclaimer applies to any damages or injury caused by the use and application, whether directly or indirectly, of any advice or information presented, whether for breach of contract, tort, negligence, personal injury, criminal intent, or under any other cause of action.

You agree to accept all risks of using the information presented inside this book. You need to consult a professional medical practitioner in order to ensure you are both able and healthy enough to participate in this program.

Table of Contents

INTRODUCTION 1

CHAPTER 1: BEFORE THE INTERVIEW 4

CHAPTER 2: TIPS FOR RESEARCHING THE HIRING COMPANY 10

CHAPTER 3: PRACTICE ANSWERING INTERVIEW QUESTION 18

CHAPTER 4: I WANT YOU TO GET YOUR DREAM JOB! 24

CHAPTER 5: IMPORTANCE OF HAVING GOOD INTERVIEW SKILLS 38

CHAPTER 6: TYPES OF INTERVIEWS AND COMMON SCENARIOS 44

CHAPTER 7: WHAT TO WEAR FOR THE INTERVIEW 50

CHAPTER 8: ATTITUDES & MINDSET 55

CHAPTER 9: PREPARING A JOB RESUME 72

CHAPTER 10: HOW TO BUILD A RESUME 81

CHAPTER 11: A SUBSTANTIALLY FILLED RESUME 84

CHAPTER 12: THE VOICES IN MY HEAD 91

CHAPTER 13: PSYCHOMETRIC TESTING 96

CHAPTER 14: GETTING STARTED 105

CHAPTER 15: RESEARCHING THE COMPANY AND INTERVIEWERS 112

CHAPTER 16: THE INTERVIEW BASICS 120

CHAPTER 17: THE WHIRLPOOL TOOL 134

CHAPTER 18: WHAT IS A JOB AND WHY DO WE WANT IT? 139

CHAPTER 19: THE INTERVIEW MINDSET 142

CHAPTER 20: GETTING STARTED 158

CHAPTER 21: INTERVIEW DO'S AND DON'TS 168

CHAPTER 22: ANALYZE YOUR STRENGTHS, WEAKNESSES, OPPORTUNITIES, AND THREATS 174

CONCLUSION 183

Introduction

Let's face it. No one likes to be confronted with their weaknesses or fears. The thought of meeting someone or something which is apparently stronger than us has the ability to make most individuals fall to their knees quaking with fear. Unfortunately, this unsettling occurrence is part and parcel of a process that, anyone who wishes to land a job, has to confront.

That's right. This dreaded event is none other than the all-important job interview process. But you might be surprised, while some loathe the interview process, some people actually relish the opportunity. Know what the difference between the two groups of people I've mentioned is? The former are the ones who face this apparently terrifying ordeal without being prepared, while the latter are usually those who have a good idea of what to expect!

According to a recent study conducted by Accounttemps, a Robert half company, forty three percent of chief financial officers who conducted several interviews believed that the job interviewing stage was where candidates made the most mistakes during the hiring process.

Max Messmer, chairman of Accountemps said "Hiring mistakes are costly to businesses, and employers are increasingly wary of choosing someone who is a poor fit for a job. The job interview can provide the best insight into whether someone is a good match."

The great playwright, William Shakespeare once said: "The world is a stage and all of us the actors, are merely players with roles to play." If we compare the nervous job applicant to an actor, then the interview room and potential employees can be considered his/her stage and audience respectively.

Why? That's because a job interview is an act in which the interviewees are merely players. If you know your lines and parts, then, hats off to you, you'll reap the rewards of your hard work and diligence. If not, well, say goodbye to that executive position and those mouth watering benefits that you've always wanted.

Chapter 1: Before The Interview

You wouldn't expect your favorite football team to go straight to the Super Bowl without practice or playing the regular season, nor should you go straight to an interview without some preparation. In fact, it might seem strange to think, but most of your interview hard work and effort actually takes place before you ever say a word to your interviewer.

One of America's first great entrepreneurs, Benjamin Franklin put it this way, "By failing to prepare, you are preparing to fail."

So let's get started!

Cover Letters

Cover letters are many people's least favorite part of the job search, an unnecessary evil they're forced to conform to due to some long-lost ancient tradition initiated in a bygone era. While they do take a little extra time and effort, think of them as your one shot. If you don't say something important or impressive, you'll never make it to the coveted interview where you can dazzle potential employers.

It might help to think of your cover letter as your 2-minute story. Nothing is less interesting to an employer than a boring cover letter. You know the type…

Dear Sir or Madame, I am writing in regard to the job posted on…**yuck!**

If you don't want to read it, why would they? If you were forced at gunpoint to read something like that, would you remember it? Accept for the odd scenario, it's doubtful you'd remember any of the letter.

A cover letter should be interesting, exciting, inspirational, possibly funny, or convey something that sets you apart from everyone else. It's your written ad selling your services.

Think about the opening line of a good book, inspirational song, or your favorite movie. They all did something to make you want to know more. Employers want to read something that makes them want to know more too.

A Word About Must-Haves

A cover letter should always be addressed to a specific human being. Never ever **To whom it may concern**, or **Dear Sir or Madame**. If you do this, you might as well throw the letter or email in the trash. No one wants to read that. If you don't bother to find out who the employer or person in charge of hiring is, why should they bother to find out who you are?

When you address your cover letter to a human, even if it isn't correct person, you're holding that person accountable to either read it or pass it on to the rightful owner. It also demonstrates to the employer that you can problem solve, research, and self-start. The simple act of putting a name on your cover letter demonstrates that you have skills they need.

While your enclosed resume states your qualifications, don't assume that an employer will read it. Make sure to list a few qualifications in the cover letter. The goal is to make things as easy as possible for a potential employer. If you have something you want them to see or something you're incredibly proud of, either provide the exact link (and double check to make sure it works), or include an attachment or copy of that important project.

Bill Gates once joked he would always hire the laziest person he could find, because they would find the easiest way to get the job done. While he might have been only half kidding, it's not wise to get lazy with most employers before the job even starts. Especially in the initial stages of your contact, your job is to make things as easy as possible for them.

Never ever tell an employer to Google you or your work. The less work for them, the better chance for you.

Finally, after all your hard work crafting the perfect letter, make sure to include your contact information. Always provide a phone number as well as an email and street address. If you have a website, include it as well.

The majority of your cover letter should be devoted to your story. Remember, like the first line of a good book or opening scene of a movie, you want something that will grab and hold a potential employer's interest. This is a great place to demonstrate some of your soft skills, (which will be covered later in this book) such as creativity, persuasion, or collaboration.

Some great ways to open a letter include a mutual contact or friend, a short story that highlights one of your traits or successes the employer might be seeking, or an anecdote or quote that relates to the position, or something that exemplifies your passion for the position or field of work. Most employers are in their jobs because they really like what they do. It makes sense that they'd want to surround themselves with like-minded individuals who share their passion.

Renee West, the President and C.O.O. of the Excalibur Hotel & Casino in Las Vegas put it well when she said, "You can have the best strategy and the best building in the world, but if you don't have the hearts and minds of the people who work with you, none of it comes to life."

Make sure to keep the cover letter brief. To be honest, most employers know by the end of the first paragraph if they're interested in hearing more from you. There's no reason to go on for more than a page. And please don't try the smaller font or decreasing the margins tricks. We know them. We've tried them. Move on.

If you would like up-to-the-minute information in a quick, easy-read format, read our other book in this series, "Land That Job! Write Captivating Cover Letters with No Silly Mistakes," by Becky Gosky.

Chapter 2: Tips For Researching The Hiring Company

You would have heard by now that it is essential to have some questions for the interviewer while interviewing for a job. Giving the hiring manager the impression that you are curious and interested in the company is great. However, you also need to have a good baseline of knowledge about the organization. You will no doubt learn more about the company in the course of the interview – information about the company culture – and you will be able to ascertain whether the company is a good fit for you.

However, it is not possible for you to have the necessary information about the company during the interview. Instead, you need to know all about the company before the interview. It is no longer challenging to learn about an employer before the interview, so plan to learn as much as you can online. However, what are the things you should be looking for when researching the company?

Things to Research about the Hiring Company

Apart from knowing where to get the information about the company, you also need to identify the essential things you need to know. Consider the following items when researching the company:

The Products, Clients and Services of the Company - Discovering the kind of work you will be doing when you are hired is crucial. You will improve your chances of success during the interview when you know about the company's products, services and clients.

Find out about the Company's Values, Mission and Culture - According to a Millennial Branding study, about 43 percent of Human Resources professionals are of the view that cultural fit is the most crucial quality that job seekers need during the hiring process. So, while researching the employer, endeavor to discover the things written about the company's mission and values. The social media networks are the best places to find out more about the culture of the company.

The Experience and Skills the Company Appreciates - Find out what the company is searching for in their ideal candidate so you can position yourself as the most qualified candidate for the position. You can find out by reading between the lines of their job descriptions and on the employer's career page.

Where to get more Information about the Company

Check the Company Website

The best place to start is the website of the company. You will be able to review their mission statement, products, and services, history, management and information about the company culture. You can get the information in the "About us" section of the website. Also, try to focus on specific themes that come up several times on the site. You will be able to find useful clues about the corporate values in the words the company used.

Are you willing to work in an organization where they consider their colleagues as family, or you need a distance between your personal life and your job? You can find out such information by going through their values. Although organizations make use of hyperbole when describing themselves, it is usually a telling hyperbole.

Search the Social Media

Most companies have social media accounts, so visit their Facebook page, Twitter pages, Instagram and Google+. You will have a better view of how the company wants their customers to see them. To get updates, simply like or follow the company. It's an excellent opportunity to uncover some "red flags" too about the company, for instance, if the company lacks a professionally managed social media presence or if their social media presence is inconsistently updated, then they might not have total control of their public image.

Check LinkedIn

One of the best places to know more about a company is via LinkedIn company profiles. You will have access to some information such as your connections at the company, jobs posted, new hires, related companies, promotions and company statistics. In case you have contacts in the company, then you might consider reaching out to them.

They can actually put in a good word for you and further share their perspective on the hiring company with great tips that will enhance your chances of success. Do you know the interviewer's LinkedIn account? Why not to check out his/her profile? You will have insight into the kind of job they are doing as well as their background. Are you in the same groups, whether online or offline? Did you attend the same school? You can easily establish rapport with the interviewer with such information.

Have an Interview Edge

You can also check up the company on Glassdoor. You will find a goldmine of information for job seekers on their interview questions and review section. Glassdoor will provide you with details of the company, which you will not find on their website. You will find information about employee functions, salary figures, company details about the hiring process, company reviews and several other crucial information.

One of the benefits is that you will discover what the interviewer asked applicants who were interviewing for the same position and get good advice on the nature of the interview. You can get a sense of company culture from the reviews. However, remember to be careful when checking the reviews because employees will still leave a great review even when they are not satisfied. Consider repeated themes when checking the reviews because the more you identify a repeated subject, the more accurate it is likely to be.

Make use of Google and Google News
Research the company name on Google News and Google. You may get invaluable information about the activities of the

company, for instance, it is possible that the company is expanding to Africa or obtained a start-up funding recently. You may also discover a new product that was recalled or underperformed. You will take advantage of this information when responding to interview questions.

What about the Industry Competitors?

Yes, it is crucial to research the industry competitors and the overall industry. For example, if you are interviewing for a position in a mortgage company, knowing the current trends about home ownership will be helpful. Who are the biggest competitors of the company? Get to know about them; find out about their successes as well as their flaws. Knowing about the company's industry and rivals will significantly impress the interviewer.

Take advantage of Your Connections

Is there anyone you know that works in the company? Ask for help. You can also ask your career office if it is possible for them to give you a list of alumni who currently work there if you are a college graduate. When you get their contact, email them or send them a message via LinkedIn for assistance.

How do you Make Use of This Research?

Hiring managers ask candidates several questions during the interview to know more about the candidate. However, their main aim of asking the questions is to ascertain whether a candidate will perfectly fit a position in the company. Therefore, your company research will definitely improve your responses to the questions and make them compelling.

It will prove to the interviewer that you will be helpful in achieving their goals and bottom line. If for instance you're asked why you want to work in the company, you can provide a specific answer and share details of the things you admire about the company, its culture, and mission.

Chapter 3: Practice Answering Interview Question

This is one of the most important part of the interview process, answering questions. As an interviewer, I have watched people absolutely struggle trying to answer questions. If you have been to a few interviews, you should have heard at least a few questions asked over and over. Think of those questions and how you plan on responding to questions you have heard in the past.

What is your greatest weakness? Sound familiar? It's one question that makes people freeze up, sweat, stare at the ceiling, show a sign of giving up, and flat out lie when they try to convince the interviewer they do not have a weakness. We all have weaknesses but how we describe them can be a deciding factor at an interview. If a person cannot handle the stress of one question, how can they handle the available job position? That's the question interviewers might be thinking when candidates that cannot provide responses to this question.

The goal to mastering the answer about your weaknesses is to minimize a weakness by tying in a strength. Remember it is a job interview so refrain from discussing personal information and direct the response towards overcoming your professional weaknesses.

One example of a weakness is being a people pleaser at work. You can turn that weakness around by stating that you were a people pleaser at work in the past, but now you have learned to become more assertive working in a team environment and focus on prioritizing tasks from urgent to the least urgent tasks to finish.

A bad way to answer that question is to say that you are a workaholic and it has taken a toll on your life. As you boost about how hard you work doing everything at work, how much overtime you have clocked, how you are rarely home for dinner with your family because of work, how much stress you are under because of work, and what medications your doctor prescribed, the interviewer is not viewing your response the same as you.

If you are right out of school and have not had a previous job, this can be tailored to school. Instead of focusing on how you were a people pleaser at work in the past, you can explain how you were a people pleaser with various activities. You learned to be more assertive with your friends and team members while working in a group or team environment, and you began to prioritize your activities from what you valued as most important after you completed your school work to the least important activity.

Another weakness that offers a response that can intertwine a strength is a fear of public speaking. Public speaking is a fear that is shared by quite a bit of people. This can be answered by saying how you have a fear of public speaking even when it's in front of a group of coworkers or classmates. You have learned how to overcome this fear by joining Toastmasters or something similar. You can also answer that you have learned how to overcome this fear by volunteering more to speak in front of your coworkers or classmates since each time you speak you have become more comfortable with public speaking. This is turning a weakness into a strength.

How do you respond to being asked a question about where do you see yourself in five years from now? The interviewer does not want to know about your goal to run a marathon, how many kids you plan to have or how you are planning on moving to a particular community. They are wanting to see how your long-term goal will apply to the job position. Your response should reflect your desire to grow your employment skills and continue your career path with the company in the next five years.

Are you ready to answer a question about why you are leaving your current job? If you're not a student, interviewers want to know an answer to this question. This does not mean they are asking you to tell them how you can't stand your current boss or coworkers. They do not want to know that you are looking to make more money and how you heard they don't work on weekends. Responding that it is closer to your home or school is not a response to provide the interviewer. They want to hear how you are seeking to further grow your skills or how the position advertised better matches existing job skills. They want a response that tells them how you leaving your current job will be a better investment for both them and you.

These have been just a few responses to interview questions. Practice how you plan on responding to questions. Remember to always respond with an answer that ties into the job position you are seeking and your strengths as an employee. Practice with a friend or family member answering the questions so that you can receive feedback from them and you will know which questions you can answer quickly and which questions you are having difficulty providing responses. Here are additional sample questions:

Tell me about yourself?
Why should we hire you?
Tell me about a problem you've faced at work, and how you dealt with it.
What's your dream job?
Why were you fired?
What's your management style?
How would your boss (professor) describe you?
What are your salary requirements?
Do you have any questions for us?
How has your education prepared you for your career?
How do you handle failure?
How do you deal with stress?

You can type the question into the search engine of your choice and find multiple web sites and blogs that provide answers. Also, Monster.com and CareerBuilder.com offer potential questions and suggested answers for interviews. The questions listed above are just a few standard questions.

Chapter 4: I Want You To Get Your Dream Job!

I want to help you apply for and get the job you want. My name is Peter Jones. I am a successful entrepreneur. One of my passions in life aside from growing businesses and making money, is seeing young people grow and develop in their careers. I also believe older people have a lot to offer the work place too. My intention in writing this book is that after reading this book, everyone will find a job. Remember it might not be your ideal job to start, but be a good employee, work hard and ethically, dream big and the world is your oyster. I really want this book to make a difference in the lives of those who read it and put my advice into practice.

We often need to employ new staff and I and my team have found this to be a hugely frustrating experience. It does not matter how big a business gets, or how many staff we have, I ideally like to interview all staff, even if I briefly meet the applicant at the last interview that takes place. As a business we tend to place our own ads online for new staff and do the interview processes ourselves. After having dealt with a number of recruitment agencies and not finding good applicants through them, we now place our own ads for new staff and do all the interviewing ourselves. But job seekers make this process so frustrating. Many just do not follow the most basic instructions. Many applicants don't even prepare for the interview and many don't even visit our company website. There are basic spelling mistakes in the covering letter and resume and the list of errors goes on. I recall applying for my first job at a law firm after getting my law degree. I checked and checked and checked my spelling and grammar again and again. I do not see this same standard of care in job applications now days.

We usually get 1000's of applications for each job ad placed online and it is clearly evident that most people don't know how to write an application email. For this reason alone, most people do not make the first interview. So what is the secret to getting an interview?

Write a good application letter, follow the instructions that the employer sets out and you have a much greater chance of getting an interview. Be honest, check your spelling and grammar.

Persevere, don't get despondent. Follow my advice, get that interview, get that job and feel and see a huge change in your life, because you know what? Work is fun! As I heard someone say recently, there is dignity in work and indeed there is. We all love holidays, but work is really fulfilling. I love that I can afford holidays in the best places in the world. Sure, work sometimes feels like a treadmill, but work is great.

So here's to many people in the world reading this, and particularly those with no hope, but loads of potential, just go for it!! And approach companies who don't have job adverts out there. Often businesses need staff, but advertising and interviewing applicants takes a huge amount of time, so apply for jobs where there are n interviews advertised., Apply for jobs at companies where you think you would like to work. Also apply for jobs at smaller companies. Many people only apply for jobs at big corporates, but many "small" businesses are booming and small businesses get big!

Make an effort in your cover letter. If you don't make an effort in your job application letter, then you surely won't make an effort in your job either! A business coach once told me, "How you do anything is how you do everything."

I really hope that you get your job. If you follow my advice, you should have success in getting your job. My advice to you is to go for it. Don't think that you cannot get the job of your dreams, believe in yourself and work hard. Remember, hard work equals good luck. And please also remember that maybe your first job won't be your ideal job, but how many people in the world just wake up to their ideal job? You actually have to do some hard work, have the right attitude and you will succeed. Be willing to learn. And I also need to emphasize this, really have a great can- do attitude.

When you get that job, be an ethical and loyal employee. By that I mean be honorable, if you ever leave, don't be a thief and take the client list or steal information you should not. We do not hire anyone who offers to bring their company's client list with them. I don't want people like that working for me. I want ethical people who I can trust.

I am now an entrepreneur but qualified as a lawyer and worked in corporate liability insurance for many years. I hated my job, but did not think that I could get a job in another industry easily. I thought that I was too involved in one industry and my legal and insurance experience would limit me. I could not afford to leave my job to study full time, so I started studying marketing in the evenings, progressed to a marketing job and then started my own business 2 years later. I think back to all those years when I did not have the confidence to apply for jobs outside of law. I had great qualifications, but they were in law and not marketing. Yet, I was a high achiever, captained many sports teams, was always in the top academic class, easily passed my law degree, qualified as a lawyer and took a job in liability insurance which I hated. But I always thought that I could not work in marketing because I had not studied it. How silly! Now days for many jobs, like marketing and other business administration jobs, you just need aptitude, a willingness to work hard, a great attitude and there you go. You can do online courses for free too. Looking back, I realize I should have applied for more jobs, spoken to more people and just taken earlier action. I had a far better education than most, was a fast learner and had a willingness to learn and start at the bottom.

But back to the job application process;

So for example my company will place an ad that reads, "Internal Sales Staff Required" and the description of what we are looking for. We would then say, please email a brief CV to Helen and advise in no more than 3 sentences why you would be the perfect person for this job. Please also advise what you would like to earn. So the reason we word this application like this is to see if applicants could follow instructions.

• Many applicants either say To whom it may concern or don't address the application to anyone at all. We have requested that they address their application to Helen.

• Some type no email at all, merely just attach their CV's.

• Others type an email much longer than 3 sentences.

• Many forget to attach their CV.

• Many have spelling errors.

• Many do not say what they would like to earn.

The reason I add the salary question is I don't want to waste my time or the applicants if their required salary is too much more than we want to pay. But those who do state it and are within our required range will get interviewed first.

So when I am going through the applications, we will simply delete the applications of those who cannot follow instructions. If they cannot follow instructions to apply for the job, then how will they actually follow instructions when doing the job?

Some applicants will say in their application email, "I know that you asked for only 3 sentences to describe why I would be the ideal applicant, but that is impossible to do, so I am going to do it in a few paragraphs." So this type of employee I bet will not easily follow instructions in the workplace either. When I say 3 sentences, I am doing this to see if the applicant can follow instructions.

Spelling mistakes are unacceptable as Google spellcheck can correct this, so if someone has not bothered to check their spelling, their application will not be considered.

CVs and Resumes (different countries use different words here)

- When writing up your CV, be honest. This is IMPORTANT.

• Also ensure that your CV is up to date.
• Keep it simple.
• Add dates of employment periods, i.e. 1 June 2016 to 15 December 2018. Don't just say 2018. Then I wonder why the person is leaving out details.

Interviews:

Preparation is vital for your interviews.

• Make sure you have gone onto the company's website and that you have researched the business. It is HUGE stupidity not to do this. Why would you not? The other day I interviewed a web developer who had not bothered to go onto our company's website before the interview. How stupid can you be?

• Know exactly what the business does

• If I interview someone who has not even been onto our website, they are wasting my time and theirs. This just shows a complete lack of preparation and we do not want people who cannot be bothered to make an effort working for us

• Be on time, well dressed, be polite.

• Have a great posture. You would be surprised by how many people are slouchy

and cannot even stand up straight or sit up straight.
- Tell us why you want to work for us.
- Tell us that you will deliver.
- Most job applicants are only interested in what you can do for them, what they can learn. Sure, but what is in it for the employer?
- Follow up with a thank you email. 99% of applicants don't bother to do this.
- Let us know afterwards if you REALLY want the job. We will be more inclined to hire someone who really wants to work with us. Do not give up, follow up weekly. Follow up, follow up, follow up.

Honesty is always paramount. I don't mind someone not being perfect for the position advertised if they state this, but if they say that they are willing to learn, I will certainly consider them. There is a saying, "hire for attitude, train for skill." So if you don't have the necessary qualifications, be honest. As a business, we are always looking to train staff and make a difference in their lives. Attitude and a willingness to work are paramount. Team work is also important. I am continuously surprised by how many people do not easily want to help their fellow colleagues. My company has a great teamwork spirit and those that cannot fit into that, at some stage or other will leave.

Reading and using this book is your first step to getting that interview and then the job.

I am constantly amazed at how sloppy, under-prepared and naive some people are when it comes to job interviews. This is a critical step in changing or progressing in your career - please don't leave it to chance.

When you do your advance research and you are fully prepared for your interview you can be more relaxed during the meeting itself. You will be more natural; less stressed and you can allow your innate personality to shine.

When you are prepared for your interview - it shows.

Then, you can meet your new employer as their absolute best candidate and be the solution to their staff search. Research the company you are interviewing at, very very very well. I cannot overemphasize this enough. And then tell the interviewer how you can add value.

In summary, show that you really want the job, be hungry, determined and have perseverance. Of course, please apply for jobs that you know you can do. You don't want to say you will be the best analyst and your knowledge is limited. Be honest. If you need some training, say so.

Remember the saying, and I repeat it, employers often hire for attitude and train for skill. I am a firm believer in the fact that we all create our own luck. Often I hear people saying, "oh so-and-so got lucky" but usually that person did not suddenly get lucky and have the perfect job fall into their lap. They might have studied hard, got good results, applied for jobs persistently, got the job and worked very hard. Remember the Gary Player saying, "the harder I practice, the luckier I get." Gary Player is a famous golfer and someone once said he hit a lucky shot and he replied, "funny that the more I practice, the luckier I get."

Many applicants also say in their covering letter that by working for us, they will gain experience in the industry etc. etc. so why the job will be good for them, but what employers want to know, is how will you add value to our organizations? Will you save us money, will you put great systems in place, are you a great motivator, have you got a great track record of increasing sales exponentially? So what can you do for us? Are you great at technology? Can you make us more efficient? Will you do great sales? Will you be an income generator for the business? Remember, you have to cover your salary.

Be positive, be enthusiastic.

Whatever you do, do it well, but don't do nothing! Be proactive. Enjoy my book and I hope that this book makes a positive difference in your life. Here's to you! My intention is writing this book is to inspire you to go out there and get that job. And if your academic qualifications aren't that great, then show what you can do with a great attitude and great work. You need to be the person who adds profit to the bottom line of the company. You make a difference. And once you have that job, be the person who volunteers to help do the stock take on a Saturday. Be that salesperson who makes that one extra call.

Chapter 5: Importance Of Having Good Interview Skills

Before we begin, here are some other resources which I recommend looking into. Although I am not a fan of their sales pages, the products themselves contain really good information.

Killer Interview Secrets

Interview Answer Guide

There is certainly a great deal of competition present in the employment world these days, and employers find themselves scanning through the paperwork of endless applicants in search of those few that they feel are qualified to move on to the next level, the crucial phase of interviewing. Those who present with a professional resume and well-written cover letter are sure to stand out far above the others. Once recognized, the distinguished candidates who successfully obtain the attention of the candidate interviewer will then find themselves immersed in the challenging, and sometimes-rigorous interview process. This overall process affords applicants the opportunity to acquaint their interviewer with their professional and personal ethics, while sharing with them their strengths, weaknesses, skills, experience, records of advancement, and career goals, in an effort to achieve success in their overall interviewing process.

The value of good interviewing skills far outweighs the perfectly written resume that reflects years and years of experience and a proven record of advancement. It's true that the applicant who submits the attractive resume along with the well-written cover letter is the applicant that, more often than not, gets noticed and earns a spot on the roster of "candidates to interview." However, earning that spot is in no way a shoe in to obtaining the position you are seeking since resumes and cover letters are truly absent personal characteristics, personality traits, work chemistry, and a personal reflection.

Though a resume does, in some form, reflect the professional individual a candidate is, and many times can confirm a candidate's skillset, years of experience, and ability to advance and better oneself, it cannot offer a potential employer insight to the person you truly are. Are you ethical? Are you dedicated and loyal? Are you ambitious and looking for advancement in your career? Are you a team player? Are you punctual, detail oriented, organized, able to streamline work, meet deadlines, and are you productive? These are all very important questions that need be answered in order for an interviewer to make a decision on whether or not a candidate fits the mold for the ideal person they are in search of, and wanting to add to their company team. A resume and cover letter certainly cannot accomplish this task, however, a personal interview can.

The Personal Interview

Personal interviews are somewhat of a gateway into the core of the candidate, many times exposing the inner person that you are and the short comings you may have, in addition to all your professional qualities. Meeting face to face, for anyone, not just a candidate and potential employer or recruiter, can be a very sensitive interaction that can cause both nervousness and anxiety for the candidate. The ability to manage these emotions in a constructive way that does not interfere with your interviewing process is, in itself, a skillset that is critical to all. When interviewing, despite your hidden fears and "jitters," a candidate must be able to separate the negative emotions from the positive presentation he must now deliver.

Staying focused on the big picture, which is simply "I really want this job" and giving no mind or focus to the apparent challenge of interacting at this level, a candidate can surprise even himself on the ability to present well, and create a positive and lasting impression. The latter is ever so important to the interview process since a positive and lasting impression is a presence that will remain etched in the mind of the interviewer. Acing a first phase interview is a confidence builder, and sets the stage for the follow up interviews with other company personnel. Recommendations made by your initial interviewer to others, will contribute greatly to the mindset of the subsequent interviewers when they are faced with the task of questioning you further in their efforts to confirm the opinions of their predecessor interviewer.

In summation, it is important to recognize the value and the impact your "perfect interview" can have on obtaining the job you are actively pursuing. Understanding the importance of the interview process, perfecting your interview skills in advance of your meeting, and keeping a clear mind, and dedicated focus on your employment goal, will set the stage and prepare you for your interview experience. Engaging in an employment interview with polished interviewing skills, coupled with confidence, and a bit of charm and wit is sure to get your interviewer to take notice. Acting professionally and naturally throughout the interview process is most assuredly a constructive approach and, if successfully executed, can find you on the receiving end of an attractive job offer, and a huge step on your personal path to professional success.

Chapter 6: Types Of Interviews And Common Scenarios

There are two main types of interviews that companies use in their interview process – Screening Interviews and Selection Interviews. Both serve the same purpose of evaluating you for the open position but they vary slightly in their approach. Most companies use both.

Screening Interviews

The first step in the interview process is typically a screening interview of some sort done by a recruiter or member of the Human Resources department. These can range from brief phone calls to tests or questionnaires that you need to submit. These types of screenings typically ask pretty basic questions to determine that you meet the minimum qualifications of the job and that you would fit in with the company's culture.

For highly technical positions they might ask you to submit examples of some of your work or ask you questions relevant to your experience to make sure you didn't lie on your application or resume. So don't lie on your application or resume! It will come back to bite you eventually.

The interviewer might ask you questions about your salary expectations or salary history. Don't stretch the truth here. If you have only been making $35,000/year but are requesting $50,000/year for the position you applied for, be prepared to say why. A good employer will pay you based on what the position is worth to them + your experience. If you don't have much relevant experience, you need to be realistic with your salary expectations or the employer won't even give you the time of day. **Do a little market research into what the position typically pays in your area so you can feel confident talking about your desired salary.** A good free source for this information is www.glassdoor.com

After you've applied for a position, be prepared for this initial phone call from your potential employer. Don't screen calls because you don't recognize the number, don't sound like you're in the middle of nap (even if you are), and don't have your music bumping in the background or kids screaming all around you. Everyone knows these things happen, but do your best to excuse yourself from a noisy environment to have a quick phone call. It's ok to ask if you can call them back at a better time if you need to. You want to sound professional from the minute they speak with you and **first impressions will make or break you.**

If you've already been selected to come in for an in-person interview, chances are you've already passed the screening interview. Congratulations!

Selection Interviews

Selection interviews are the second step in the interview process and are typically done in person, though in the case of long distances they can be done via video conference. There are number of different ways these are done and depending on the position, many companies do a series of several selection interviews over the course of a few weeks to narrow down their applicant pool so it will be best for you to prepare for any and all of these scenarios. Smaller companies often select their candidate after only one interview.

Group

Group interviews are very rare. However, if you applied to a company that has several openings for the same position or a position where you will work with a team at all times you might encounter this type of interview. You will be placed with another candidate or several candidates and interviewed together. The goal here is for the interviewer(s) to assess how you interact in a group setting. Are you a follower or a leader? Are you assertive or aggressive? Are you a talker or a listener? How do you react in stressful situations? These are some of the things determined in a group interview. There is no reason to stress yourself out about this, you've already been selected for this, so they have liked you up to this point. Now just show them more of what they might see if you were hired.

Panel

Typically there are several people involved in deciding whether or not you'll be hired and in a panel interview all of those people involved are in the room to interview you together. Don't worry, they put their pants on the same way you do in the morning. Shake all their hands and make eye contact when they are speaking. There might be a "speaker" of the group who asks you the majority of the questions; avoid speaking only to that person. Direct your answers or questions to the entire group, not just one person.

Panel interviews are common and can be very intimidating if you aren't prepared. Consider this a test of how you work under pressure, so stay calm and be yourself. The interviewers know how nerve wracking it can be and many times they will try to make you feel comfortable by breaking the ice with non-job related chit chat to start with.

One on One

One on One interviews are the most common interviews and probably the least stressful. It's easier to connect with one person in the room, remember their name, make eye contact, etc. Typically the person interviewing you will likely be your direct supervisor for the position. They want to get an idea of how you would fit in their work environment and company culture. Be respectful and remember that the interviewer might have several other interviews lined up so be sure to present the best version of yourself.

Chapter 7: What To Wear For The Interview

When you attend a job interview you want to look professional and like you are going to fit into the company. For men a shirt and tie or a suit is always a safe choice, but for women, picking the clothes is a little more challenging. Both men and women should pick an outfit that you feel comfortable in and that fits you properly. You should not wear pants that are too tight or a shirt that is too snug across the chest. Try to choose colors that suit you but aren't too bright or patterns that are not overly bold. Many women prefer to wear a black or blue suit. Ultimately you want the focus to be on your answers, not what you are wearing.

Be cognizant of the fact that your overall appearance is going to be judged, and this includes more than the clothes you are wearing. Always be clean, neat and tidy. It is not recommended that you wear a strong scent – chances are you will be in a small room and it could make others uncomfortable. The length of your finger nails should be medium to short and clean. Your hair should be styled appropriately and avoid any wild or outrageous hair do's. It's wise to have mints with you or brush your teeth immediately before leaving for the interview. The details of dressing appropriately has a lots to be with getting the job specifically if you are going to be dealing with the company's customers face-to-face. The company will want to hire employees who are going to represent the company in the best possible light.

Make Contact With References Before Interview

It's important to find out how a former employer viewed you and your work history with them. Even if your memory of your time spent in a position is positive, you don't know how you were remembered or what will be said unless you ask. Your first step should be to contact everyone that you are considering using as a reference. You should confirm if they are working for the same company and if their phone number is the same. If a boss has moved to another company, you can still utilize them as a reference provided you can track them down.

When you reach a potential reference, don't assume they will remember you and everything about you – remind them. Things you reference during your conversation can have a positive outcome on what they have to say about you later. Ask if they are comfortable providing you with a favorable reference and if there is any feedback they have for you. If you are very comfortable you can ask how they felt about your time working with them and what they would say about you if someone called to ask. If you are not comfortable with providing a direct supervisor or boss you can use other employees in the company that old a supervisory position. Think of people you have worked closely with on projects or such – they are valid and reputable people to provide as references too. If you have made it through the interview process, a reference would have to go quite badly for it to affect a possible job offer.

Poor Working Relationship With Your Boss
Bad relations with your boss may be the reason you are looking for another job in the first place, but how do you approach this situation so it will not hinder your chances at a new company? There are a few steps you should take first and you need to mind what you say during the interview. A lot of interviews will contain at least one question about your working relationship with your current boss. They can take many forms and you should prepare for a lot of different types of questions that may be asked. No matter what the question, even if it is one asking you to describe conflict with your boss, be positive and do not bash anyone in your answers.

Make every effort to remove any emotions from the equation and explain the situation using the facts and highlight all of the professional steps you have taken to rectify the situation. Don't try and make your boss sound like the bad guy, and try to de-emphasize the entire event. It may seem like an opportunity to vent about the situation but if you do, your are cutting off an avenue to escape the working relationship you want to get away from. Present the facts, be neutral and highlight your problem-solving skills. If you are concerned that your current boss will sabotage your efforts to find another job during the reference check stage you can solve this in a couple of ways. If your boss is reasonable and the two of you just don't work well together, chances are you don't have to worry too much. Be sure to give him or her heads up though. If you aren't comfortable with this, try and find another manager that you have worked for in the company previously that you can pass on as a reference.

Chapter 8: Attitudes & Mindset

In order to set ourselves up for the best possible success, we need to adopt the proper mindsets and understand where we are, where we want to go and how we are going to get there. Just like going on a cross country trip, you would start off without a map or in these days, a GPS! You are going to draw your own map and this book is going to be your GPS.

Below we are going to list a few different subjects pertain to the employment process. Most of this content you already know but our intention is not to show you anything earth shattering new but instead to get you to look at them in an entirely different manner. Because when we look at things differently, we often understand them more and change our behavior towards them.

With that in mind here are 4 things you need to examine before we get started:

It's a Competition – Never Forget That!

Most people think of the employment and interview process as an evaluation process. By that I mean people think that applicants send in their resumes and companies look at them to see if they have the qualifications and education to do the job. If they have what the company requires, they are asked in for an interview.

If that's how you look at the process, then you are wrong and you probably are limiting yourself in your resume and during interviews. Here is how you can correct all of this quickly and easily. You just have to change the way you look at the process.

This entire process is a competition. What the company wants or demands from you is the BARE MINIMUM that you need to have to even be considered. The bare minimum does not guarantee you an interview! It just gets you considered!

Your resume and performance at interviews is going to be measured against other applicants with qualifications similar to yours. Some might be better and others might be worse. But the people who get into the interview phase are thought of as the best overall performers. That means your resume impressed certain people more than other resumes did.

You might not be the best candidate but your resume portrayed you to be. You might not have the best education or experience but your performance at the interview convinced someone you were the right one for the job. This is all a competition and you are completing against everyone who sent in a resume or responded to an on-line job posting.

This is an important viewpoint because when we look at anything as a competition we soon begin to find ways to give ourselves an unfair advantage. Just like athletes make subtle changes to gain an extra tenth of a second or run a bit faster to outrun their opponents, you will soon be looking for any advantage you can think of to make yourself look better and more impressive in the eyes of others.

Imagine your resume out on a table with 20 other resumes and the top6 get chosen for an interview. Picture interviewers getting together at the end of the day to compare notes on the applicants they interviewed that day. 10 people might have been interviewed with the top 4 going on for a second interview.

Will you be one of those ones who get chosen for the interview or go on for the second interview? Will you be the one who recognized that this is a competition and that every applicants is doing their very best to make themselves look as good as they possibly can. Are you the person who does everything they can possibly do so they get the opportunities others fall short of?

Think of this entire process as a competition where the one who comes out on top gets the job. Not the one with the best education or the most experience. But the one who beats out everyone else and convinces people that they, not anyone else, represents the best fit for the position.

Once you do that, your mindset towards a lot of little things will change dramatically.

Yourself as the Product

This is where a lot of people might have a problem. For many people thinking of themselves as products is despicable. Equating themselves to a box of laundry detergent or a pair of slacks is not something they feel comfortable with. But when you really look at it, that description is very accurate when applied to the employment process.

Think about it for a minute. The consumer (the company that is hiring) is looking for something to solve a problem (doing a job or providing knowledge or skills). So the person they are going to hire is the product that will provide that knowledge, skill sets or other value. IN that sense the person being hired can be thought or as a product.

Now let's turn it around a little bit differently and look at it from the applicant's point of view. IN this view you have many "products" being considered to solve a specific problem. Just like going to the store to figure out which brand or model will best suit your needs, the resume and interview process is where all the applicants "products" are being evaluated to see which one will be purchased (hired).

Once you understand this and can think of yourself in that manner, your thought process changes as you create your resume and prepare and perform at interviews. It is all about making you appear to be the best product for the job. Once you can feel comfortable with that, you are home free.

Your Personal Sales Pitch

Now that you can think of yourself as a product, let's take a look at how you are going to market yourself to various companies. This involves creating your personal "sales pitch" that you will present to people at the company that you are going to interview with. This is how people will see and interact with you.

Think of your resume as an advertisement with you as the product. Your education and experience become features and benefits. Your resume shows people how effective you are in accomplishing the needed goals of the position. In other words, your resume is an advertisement that ties you into solving a specific problem for the company. The more problems your resume addresses and potentially solves, the more valuable you look as an applicant.

The interview is your personal "infomercial" where you get to show others how good you are in person or on camera. Your interview takes the words and print on your resume and brings them to life. Your interview is where people get to see and get acquainted with the product and to see and learn things they can't see in a resume.

It is important to realize that everything you do from the initial application to the last interview is one long and detailed sales pitch with you as the product. This might sound a bit crude or crass but it is a very accurate way of looking at the process. Once we look at it in this manner we see the need and advantage of crafting our sales pitch in a very specific and targeted way.

Many others are doing this for their candidacy, shouldn't you be doing it as well?

Getting to the Interview

Last, but certainly not least, there is one more attitude that we must change if we are to be at our most successful selves. That attitude is that most of the work goes into the resume to get us selected and once that is accomplished, the rest is a piece of cake. We need to get rid of that mindset right away.

Yes, the resumes should be designed with its sole purpose to make you appear to be the perfect candidate for the position you are applying for. Every line item should be worded with that intent in mind. Every bit of research should help you identify the right content and the right phrasing. But this is just step one in the process.

Once the resume has worked its magic and resulted in a call or letter stating that you have been selected for an interview, the net phase of work and preparation takes effect. This is where you have to take things to the next level and make sure you are ready for the interview.

Consider the interview as a live resume or sorts. This is where you get talk about what is in your resume and draw the parallels and make the connections between what the company wants and what you have to offer. This is where you get to convince someone in real time.

But there are a few differences and these differences both point to an even greater need for research and preparation. Here are two of the most important ones:

An Interview is Longer

If you were to read your resume all the way through it would probably take less than 5 minutes. But let's say it did take 5 or even 10 minutes for someone to read everything that was in your resume. An interview might be 30 minutes long or possibly longer depending on the job you are applying for. That means there will be a lot more information being discussed during your interview than there was on your resume.

All of that information is going to come from the questions are going to be asked. Questions that are going to require knowledge and thought and some careful research and preparation. So don't think that just knowing your resume and being prepared to discuss what is in it will get you through the interview. That information is important but it is a fraction of what you will be asked in the interview.
An Interview is Live!

When you created your resume you crated a rough draft and then refined it, changed things around, changed the wording or phrasing and did a lot of other things to make your final copy much, much better and more effective than that original draft. You had time, you had privacy and you were able to think and re-evaluate things as you went along.

Your interview, however, is going to believe. You are going to sit in front of someone, or some people, and you are going to have to think on your feet and come up with answers, good answers, right then and there. You are not going to be able to say something, realize you could have said it better and then take it back and say it again.

You are performing live, with no tape delay and, as circus performers might say, without a net.

So if your plan is to walk in with your resume and field questions on the fly and just say what pops into your head, you might want to rethink that approach. Depending on the job you are applying for, you might be going up against seasoned pros who have been coached and educated and prepared for what is coming. If you don't do the same you are not likely to get the best results.

An Interview Can Be Stressful

I am not trying to scare anyone here but interviews are designed to be somewhat stressful. So you need to get exposed to a bit of stress so you know how to deal with it and react. You want to appear calm and controlled on the outside even though your stomach is churning on the inside. All of this comes through preparation and knowing what is likely to come next.

This way you can calm down, think straight and be at your best. Your answers will be clearer, your impression will be stronger and you will get further in the process as well.

It might surprise you that the entire interview process is more mental than anything else. People who are able to deal with the mental and emotional aspect of the interview often have a huge advantage over those who are scared or intimidated by it. That is why this book is going to help you so much if you give it the chance.

If you will allow your viewpoints to shift a little bit and if you are receptive to looking at some things in different ways you can ace any interview that might come your way. If you know what to expect and how to come up with the right answers to tough questions and when to say the right things at the right time you can go far.

We are now going to get into how to prepare for your interview. In many respects this is the most important part of the process because what is done at that point will shape how you impress and perform from that point on. So pay close attention, even to the little things, and start preparing for the next interview that comes you way.

Because if you ace that one, it could be years before your next one!

You Need Them More Than They Need You!

We need to get one thing understood really early in the process because some people think this is an even process. That the company needs you as much as you need them. They also think that the company should be equally concerned with what's important to you as you are in what is important to them.

To both of those opinions I say HOGWASH! (Which is a nice way of saying CRAP!)

Unless you are a truly unique person with special skills and talents that nobody else has, you are not as special or valuable as you think you might be. This can be hard for some of us to come to terms with. But the reality is that for every job posting there are about 100 applicants. Many of these applicants will meet the overall qualifications for the job you are applying for.

What this means is that if the company doesn't hire you they will hire someone else. That person will probably do a pretty good job and no one is going to lose sleep because you weren't hired.

I'm not saying this to make you feel bad just to give you a sense of reality and to get you to realize that it is up to you to impress them and not the other way around. You have to convince them to hire you. They don't have to beg you to come to work for them. Sometimes this might not be true but the majority of time it is.

What all of this means is that you go through the process at their invitation and mostly at their convenience. While they might bend to accommodate your schedule they pretty much tell you where to be and when. They set the standards and it is up to you to meet them, not the other way around.

This is one of those times when even the most entitled person on the planet needs to understand that the interview process is centered on you impressing other people to choose you for the job and not the other way around. Once you figure this out you will find your attitude changing for the better and you will soon see the reason and merit for doing certain things in order to make yourself look and appear better.

Throughout this book we will be making suggestions of things you can do to make yourself appear to be the better candidate. It is up to you as to whether you do them or not. But always remember it is up to you to meet their standards and not the other way around.

Don't Sell Yourself Short!

One thing many people do is sell themselves short when it comes to applying for jobs or talking about their accomplishments. But the fact is, most people apply for jobs they don't think they can really do and discover once they're in place they do just fine.

Now this doesn't mean you should apply for any job and just learn on the fly. It is one thing to apply for a job managing 100 people when the most people you ever managed was 5 and applying for a job as a brain surgeon while never going to medical school or having any medical training!

A lot of people "fake it until they make it" when taking on new jobs. As long as your comfort level is fairly high and you know how to go about learning the things you need to learn go ahead and go for it. But if you put yourself in a position where what you do can harm someone else or hurt the company, I would advise you to think twice or even three times about taking that job.

In other words, give yourself credit where credit is due and always try to stretch your capabilities and learn something new. Almost everyone is a little nervous when stepping into a new position. But don't let that stop you. Just be prepared to learn a little faster, work a little bit harder and reduce the learning curve before anyone really catches on.

Judging from some of the people I've worked with over the years, you will do just fine!

Chapter 9: Preparing A Job Resume

Job resumes to be written with the intention of securing the job. Before writing a job resume it is necessary to read and understand the job advertisement / job posting to make sure whether you possess required experience, academic /professional qualifications, job knowledge etc. If you don't have the required qualification its better avoid writing. We must ensure that the candidate has all required criteria with qualifications. There is a vast difference between Curriculum Vital and job resume. Curriculum Vital furnishes detailed information of the candidate, his interests, job functions and other personal information.

When you write a job resume you give information as requested in the advertisement or job posting. It is not necessary to state information other than requested, in a job resume. A job resume should always be accompanied with a covering letter. In the presence of

advanced communication systems in the universe, the writing fashions are changed to meet with present global requirements. Today we don't write a covering letter too long because every body is busy with their engagements and people can't afford to read lengthy letters. A covering letter should bear following information in brief.
• Sender's address
• Receiver's address
• Date
• Caption – Job position

In first paragraph it should indicate that you are submitting your application, reference to the advertisement. Then you mention your total number of years experience, competency and your desire to apply for the job. Also you can mention about your availability on job with names and details of two referees. You must say your resume is incorporated with the covering letter.

Your application will get screened and short listed in the process of selecting with the weight of it. Otherwise it will never get shortlisted. When its short listed you have a chance and a hope of going ahead facing to interviews. If the cover letter and resume works well you have to concern about preparing to the interviews that may come ahead. In this case you have to insert only the most wanted and requested information.

What to do in a job interview

This is really an irritating question to most job seekers for the first time in life. They have no experience of attending interviews. Even some experienced hands that have been stagnating in one organization meets with this problem. Such categories should be trained to face interviews. They should be educated about various stages of interviews. Smartness, neatness, developed personality will help them to a certain extent to pass at least some stages of interviews.

They should be taught about body language, interview competency, interview techniques etc.

1. Body Language

It's great if any person hoping to attend an interview to know what body language is. From the time you enter interview arena, the interview board will observe, study all your movements, body language. You have to keep in mind that a competent administrator, HR manager can get a general impression of the candidates participating in interviews, by their walk, the way they converse, how they present themselves in interview. If you get exited, blushed, twisted in front of them, they are keen to observe such lapses. When answering to their questions, you have to be extra careful, that doesn't mean that you are to get exited or alarmed. Always be smart, be pleasant and be free when conversing with interview board. In my experience I have noticed some candidates act in a very unusual manner by twisting on the chair or meddling with some article kept on the table. This type of behavior has to be avoided completely. One answer to one question would do. At any rate a candidate should not converse too much. Answer only to point. Body language depicts, how stable, how steady and whether you are settled down as an interview candidate.

2. Interview Competency

Interview candidates have to give a very close attention to details of this chapter. Interview Competency is a topic that should be discussed among superiors and managerial categories of employees. This topic is not at all banned for staff, middle management and employees but it especially applies to the primary category. Staff members, employees going through this report will get enlightened about the subject and it will definitely help them when facing job interviews.

What's Interview Competency? Chairman, CEO, MD and top managerial staff of a company should determine to appoint an Interview panel, consisting of competent personal to conduct interviews. It is an absolute truth that every body is not competent of everything. When selecting a team to serve in an Interview Panel, attention to detail, job position, and the department in which the vacancy exists&

technical competency should have to be considered to a great extent. It's very important to evaluate the members of interview board accordingly to assess their suitability to serve in the interview panel. Whenever requirements are not fulfilled, competent officers from out side can be hired. Interview competency is assessed to a very high degree in every employment sector because we have to recruit highly competent & qualified human Resources to perform in different job positions.

Supposing when we intend interviewing a technically qualified Civil Engineer, with the intention of entrusting him / her to manage a certain project, sometimes unfavorable situations may arise because we have no competent persons to serve in interview panel. In such a situation what do you propose? We have experienced that in certain companies / organizations, CEO or Chairman appoints two senior managers of the company to conduct interviews. What would be the final result? We can expect following results which are not favorable to company.

Persons appointed to serve in interview panel will be embarrassed they are not competent to serve in interview panel.

Interviewees get puzzled as the interview is not up to their expectations. Also irrelevant questions are being raised to them.

Most probably a candidate who is not competent is recruited to perform the job. Additional burden to company as he / she doesn't perform in the capacity recruited and paying his salary is a loss to company.

Now we think of solutions for such situations. We may not have any competent persons internally to serve in the interview board. Remedy is to hire an out side person with technical qualifications and interview competency. It is of immense important to have trained interview panels with expertise job knowledge and interview competency in every organization. Senior managers, Heads of Departments can be trained externally to over come the situation.

The aspect of Training & Development is adding an extra value to organizations because it will keep the cost of hiring out side officers low to a certain extent. Interview competency is absolutely important to any employment sector because competent persons are required to operate projects with semi competent staff. Interview competency should be trained and practiced in organizations from head to foot not from foot to head.

Training & Development

Since Training & Development is under the purview of Human Resources Department, HR personal should take every possible step to train staff / employees as per various requirements of the company. Hiring an out side person to serve in interview panel will cost a lot to company. Cost consciousness is a major factor that should be emphasized carefully in bringing down unnecessary costs.

HR training on various employment areas is very essential especially to new associates, when they join companies in unskilled capacities. Training gives members additional job knowledge while motivating them to enhance productivity and add values their personalities. Training makes people active and teaches them to operate in their individual capacities in high spirit and energy. Following internal trainings are very important to new comers in organizations.

- HR orientation
- Personality Development
- Team building / team spirit
- Productivity enhancement
- Motivation
- Quality consciousness

Chapter 10: How To Build A Resume

Building a resume is more than just throwing words together on a piece of paper. If you need help doing that, check out my course on resume building or contact me directly, and I'll help put together a resume for you that gets you noticed. In order to build a good resume, you need time, experience, and a little education always helps.

Having multiple resumes can be a good idea, especially if you're gaining experience in different industries. However, be sure to keep it updated and relevant to the times and those industries. If you have a career path, one resume is fine. This chapter will focus on the "one resume" approach. For more help with multiple resumes, shoot me an email on LinkedIn at any time.

Assuming you've taken the technological approach, even if you didn't, what I'm about to share with you will open your eyes to how we, as recruiters, find passive and active job seekers, like yourself, and why we end up calling them for interviews. They're called Boolean searches, algorithms designed to scour the World Wide Web and collect dozens of resumes based on key identifiers or buzzwords. This is why, when building a resume, it is important to do a little research first on the jobs you're going to be applying to. Think about your industry. What types of computer programs do you use? What certifications did you have to get? What organizations or events does your particular industry hold? All of the answers to these questions may be incorporated into building your resume. Research the job you are applying to and make a list of the skillset it requires. Your resume should be riddled and sprinkled with words from that list. This will ensure it gets seen first after having been posted online to sites like ZipRecruiter or Indeed. It will make you stand out against the competition that simply listed their previous work history and job responsibilities in bullet form from memory. Depending on the industry, a resume layout can make or break you. In some of my courses, and one-on-one training, I talk about the various types of resumes. However, for the sake of this e-book, I'm just going to describe the crucial and most important parts of a resume.

Formatting is everything when it comes to a resume. Your resume should be concise and straight to the point. You typically want to include your contact information at the top and your education last, at the bottom. Your objective, previous employment, and certifications will all go in the middle. And that's it. In two pages or less, always preferably one, you have yourself a resume. For further information on formatting and what a good resume looks like, be sure to contact me or take one of my courses online.

Chapter 11: A Substantially Filled Resume

Employers are always looking for smart recruits, which is something they can quickly judge by taking a look at the resumes of the job applicants. Simply defined, a resume is a brief overview of one's academic background, professional achievements, experiences, and personal interests. Whenever there is a job opening, most companies will require applicants to submit a resume alongside a cover letter prior to the interview. A resume helps an employer catch an invaluable glimpse of one's potential, and in some instances, employment decisions will be made based solely on this fundamental requirement. The use of a resume has become so ingrained in every employment culture across the world that even before a job opening comes up, everyone is in a rush to craft a perfect resume and have it delivered in good time once the opportunity presents itself. Essentially, a resume is a vital element for anything that relates to job application, and it is on this premise of its indispensability that people always strive to create a solid first impression by using resumes before meeting. This always takes place long before one faces a potential employer through a job interview. The question is, how can you crush a job interview using a resume and annihilate your competitors? Even though it precedes an interview, a well-written resume is sure to boost your chances of being hired even before an interview is conducted. Here are some tips that will help you to fine-tune your resume and stand a high chance of being hired.

What should appear on your resume, and what should not?

A resume is a form of self-marketing magic, a characteristic that many have more often than not overlooked. This has continued to limit the chances of many people when it comes to employment. Your resume should have value in it, which brings us to the issue of what you need to include in it and what should be left out. Most people apply for jobs that meet their personal interests, experience, and academic qualifications. This means that they will always express their interest in vacancies they feel suitable enough to take on, but while many do this, a resume that is devoid of details relating to the job in question can indicate otherwise. A resume should be short and precise, a characteristic that makes it easy for a potential employer to review. Imagine a situation in which about five hundred applicants have expressed their interest in a job opening and sent in a resume. In order to compete against time, an employer will likely spend a maximum of three minutes perusing the resumes of applicants. The use of this process to see the right person get hired will always rub a number of applicants the wrong way, especially those with unnecessarily long resumes of up to, say, twenty pages. This means that to be among the best candidates for the job, your resume should only include content relevant to the job you have applied for. For example, don't include content relating to a teaching experience if you are applying for a position in sales and marketing. Also, keep in mind that there will be people who make the mistake of applying for the same job as you using the same generic resume that they use for every other job. Exploit this weakness by tailoring your resume to the job specifically.

Resume wording and formatting

The way your resume looks can either boost your chances of getting hired or ruin your hopes completely. Thousands of people around the world, while applying for jobs, have shown little to no consideration regarding using the right words and formatting styles when compiling their resumes. If, for example, you have working experience in a technical field such as process engineering and you want to apply for a job with little to no technical aspects, then the trick is to tone down your technical wording while perfecting your formatting.

While it is suicidal to send the same old resume to tens of prospective employers, using the same format can also spell doom. This is especially true if the job opening to which you are applying requires a simple-to-follow structure and easy-to-understand language. It would be an unthinkably bad idea for an Information Technology specialist applying for a sales job to use the same IT language in the application. If this becomes the case, you can bet on ruined chances. What does your resume look like? What is the readability level of your resume? What is your choice of words? These are questions that should make you consider aspects of word document formatting, such as alignment, spacing, font type, font size, and typefaces. It is important that you use a consistent typeface, font size, and spacing, for these are the aspects that would most enhance the readability of your resume. No employer has the patience or the time to strain to read a resume that is packed with words and inconsistent in formatting. Most companies will post guidelines on the formatting styles they need to see in applications; if they do, be sure to properly follow the instructions in the job post. The aspect of language register is also pivotal if all you need out of an interview is to get an edge over your competitors and get hired. Here, you ought to take into serious consideration the level of language you use, especially with regard to terminologies. Every field is unique in terms of language, which is something you should understand before sitting down to craft a resume. Use medical language if you are applying for a job in medicine, but don't use the same language if you later apply for an IT job opening.

Resume appeal and presentation

How your resume looks is its 'appeal', and how it is delivered is 'presentation'. Are you the kind of a person who does not follow the formatting rules for word documents but still expects to be considered for a job position because you believe that you have what it takes? If you fall into this category, then you are mistaken. The same way airhostesses dress the part, so should you dress the part when it comes to crafting an appealing resume.

You will only have yourself to blame if a potential employer throws your resume into a bin because it looks awful, but remember that this is something you can easily avoid. It takes patience to craft a well-formatted resume that is sure to help you crush a job interview. This should be crowned by the way the resume is presented. How do you deliver your resume? While most companies will give guidelines for application presentation, in most cases it is left to common sense. Make sure you deliver your resume, which is usually accompanied by other documents like testimonials and cover letter, in a neat and clean envelope or folder. This is both professional and clearly communicates who you are. However, it should be noted that an eye-catching resume that is lacking in substance will still not take you anywhere near shortlisting.

Chapter 12: The Voices In My Head

"The difference between a successful person and others is not a lack of strength, not a lack of knowledge, but rather a lack of will."- Vince Lombardi

I want to take a minute out to applaud you. The reason you are already better than 90% of the other candidates is that you are doing what 70% of Americans admit they have not done in the previous 5 years. You picked up and are reading a book. You care enough to not only do your research, but you are building your skills in interviewing. It will pay off.

I want to start off by bringing you into the scary world of my brain. I am the intimidating (I love people, literally joke most of the day, and watch football on Sunday's so I always get amused when I make a candidate nervous) force on the other end of the phone, on the video feed of your computer, or across the desk from you depending on the interview. I am the one who holds the cards. I decide to push you forward or give your resume to the nice girl who keeps it on file to appease Uncle Sam and his many regulations for why we pass on a candidate.

I want you to get the chance to walk around and hear my thoughts, see what I focus on, what I could care less about, and what sways my opinion early, bad or good. You see, I am like you. I have pressure that Society has put on me. I drive a car, pay for gas, pay for my student loans, the mortgage, the Honeymoon, and the groceries. I have a job to do. I have numbers to hit. I have a responsibility to grow our Company. I want you to get the job. How funny is that? You walk into the meeting nervous and thinking that the person across from you hates you and wants to crush your chances. The honest to God truth is I want you to get hired. You walk in with a built in advantage in that it helps me and my career if you are a good candidate. So, let's show you how to be a good candidate (for your sake and mine).

Sourcing Call: This is the call that I make because you either applied to the job, had your resume online or I found you through Social Media, a Career Fair, etc. During this call I mainly care about getting you interested in us. You are basically interviewing me. What bothers me during the Sourcing call? Honestly, not much. The only way to really bother me here is if you come across rude because you do not know me and I am reaching out to you about a job.

Really? Our Economy has been in shambles, student debt is through the roof, millions cannot find work, and you decide that I am being rude for calling you about a job? I wish I were able to say that to a candidate when they act like I am purposely bothering them and trying to waste their time. No one likes or wants to be bothered and I understand that. We have all had the Uncle or friend from High school that we have not talked to in years suddenly call us to sell us knives for $1.2 million and the experience sucks. Badly. I am not that Uncle or Friend.

I am selling a potential job that you have not heard about yet. Please, be polite when you are called as you never know what the call will be about. One guy in one of the Companies I mentioned was delivering pizzas when he got his call. He made over a half of million dollars as a sales rep a few years later. Do you think he was rude on his initial call? Doubtful, and today he and his family are happy that he wasn't.

Once this call is over the real work begins assuming you are interested. You must show initiative now or I will assume you are good with what you have going on now and do not wish to proceed. How you can do this? Respond to my email requesting your resume promptly. Submit anything that I have asked for the first time I ask for it. When I ask for you availability, give me 3-4 times that work for you spread out over 2-3 days. That comes across as professional, considerate, and saves us both time of back and forth.

When you send the resume, include it in an email in which you thank me for reaching out. Save the resume as (Your) Last Name, First Name, Resume. This email can be brief but reiterate your interest in this body as this goes a long way into getting me to buy into you wanting the job. You have done your part and the next step is to prepare for the Voices in my head during the interview.

Chapter 13: Psychometric Testing

Psychometric testing refers to the process of measuring a candidate's relevant strengths and weaknesses. This form of measurement is primarily employed to assess employment suitability, including company-candidate fit. The aim of psychometric tests is to gain an accurate bearing of the candidate's cognitive abilities and personality/behavioral style.

Psychometric testing is becoming more and more popular now to vet potential candidates and you can use these in your favour. If you've never taken one before it can be a little bit worrying, it's a bit like going back to school and sitting an exam doing those multiple choice questions with puzzles! But there is basically no need to worry at all once you understand what they are for, how they work and what they are set out to achieve.

Companies have increasingly taken to using these tests to gauge applicants as nowadays there are so many well qualified applicants for each job and they had to interview them all, it would take quite some time.

These tests are a good way to assess which candidates are most likely to be the best fit for the job. If you are the right person for the position then it will just give reassurance to the interviewer and you will be in a good position.

If you have never sat a psychometric test or heard of one for that matter I will give you some brief information about them. A psychometric test isn't really a test and that is because you cannot really fail one. It is called a test because you will then be assessed on at the end. What these tests do is to ascertain how you think and whether you think in the same format as the company you are applying to but these tests don't tend to be used on their own in the interview and selection process.

Basically psychometric tests – are split into four areas and can include one or all of the following;

An Ability Test,

A Personality Test,

An Aptitude Test,
Motivational Test.

Each test speaks for itself, the ability test is looking to assess your overall general ability, the personality test is assessing what type of personality you have, the aptitude test is carried out to test the skills you have that are specific to areas of the job that you are applying for and the motivational test which is set to find out what motivates you.

Don't panic if you are on your way to an interview and you suddenly a thought goes through your head like "oh no I wonder if I will be asked to sit a psychometric test at this interview". It is very unlikely if you haven't been informed that a psychometric test will form part of the interview that it will be sprung on you – after all that would be a bit of a dirty trick to play on an unsuspecting candidate. These tests are often carried out on the same day as the interview but generally speaking you will be given advance warning if this is going to form part of the day.

Should you be asked to sit a test as part of the interview then the chances are the interviewer or the Human Resource manager will brief you beforehand as to what the test is all about, what you need to do to complete the test and which type of test you will be asked to complete. If they do not brief you (which is fairly unlikely) then you might want to ask them a few questions about the test – things like how will the test be taken, what type of test will you be taking and what will the information be used for etc.

There is plenty of information readily available about psychometric tests on the internet so if you want examples or more information on this subject just go and search for "psychometric tests". If you know you are going to be taking a test then make sure you have everything you need before attending (it's just like going into an exam without a pen or your glasses) make sure you are prepared you don't want to add to your worries by leaving something important at home that's going to hinder you. You should use the same type of formula when taking the test as you would if you were taking an exam. Here are a couple of pointers:

Sit down, keep your cool and follow all of the instructions given on the paper. Read them thoroughly and take them in. If you rush you may misunderstand the way in which the test is being set and end up answering questions incorrectly.

If at the start of the test there is an area that you are unsure of or do not fully comprehend then ask the assessor for help.

As with any exam you need to answer as many questions as possible correctly so be careful if the time spent on each question. If you are not sure of the answer or don't understand the question don't get flustered, leave it and move on, you can always return to the question again at the end if you have time left over.

Finally, if when you have finished all of the questions and there remain some unanswered ones go back and have another go and by all counts if you still don't know the answer just guess – you might come out lucky!

I will try and give you some insight into what you can expect from the different types of tests and how to answer them, I am no expert at the end of the day I can only go off my past experience and information I have read up on the subject.

Ability/Aptitude Tests:

Ability and aptitude tests are set to assess your specific skills. You will sit the test and the resultant mark you get will indicate to your future employer your overall level of ability. The content of the test may be general questions set to see how you think, how you deal with specific circumstances and what type of logic you are using to come up with your answer. These tests are frequently designed using multiple choice questions.

Sometimes these tests will be set using far more questions than can possibly be answered in the allotted time but it is quality not quantity the examiner will be looking for as your overall score will be a percentage of the right questions answered not how many questions have been answered.

It is fairly easy to do some preparation for aptitude tests, most of these tests are based around logical thinking which is something that we all do in everyday life. If you really want to try and increase your logical thinking you could try the doing the daily crossword in your newspaper, Sudoku which you can get from most local shops (or even play it on the internet for free) or you could try buying one of those puzzler magazines from WH Smiths or Sainsbury's.

What I am getting at here is that you need to get your mind working in a logical thinking way and by carrying out exercises that involve mathematical puzzles and problem solving you will give yourself a good start. Remember the more practice you get the better you will become at doing these tests.

Motivation Tests/Personality Tests:

Motivation questionnaires are set to specifically analyze what "motivates" or "drives" you as a person and how you are likely to integrate that into your work, how much stamina you have or how much enthusiasm you dedicate to a project.

These tests are likely to set using a question followed by several possible answers. Personality tests are very similar to Motivation Tests and are designed to assess what type of person you are, unlike Aptitude tests which are created to analyze what type of logic you use to address problem solving. There are no right or wrong answers to Personality tests because everyone thinks differently and these tests are designed more to see if you will fit in with the companies way of thinking or the type of job you will be doing. Generally speaking there will be no time limit set at a personality test so they are not as pressurized as aptitude tests. It is not possible to analyze what sort of information the employer is looking for when you take a personality test as different employers will be looking for different qualities and they may be aimed at how well you are going to fit into their team and company. However, the general type of areas your employer may be looking to quantify are what your attitude is to your work life and personal life, how well you communicate with others, what drives you and how you deal with sorting out and solving problems.

Chapter 14: Getting Started

Understand Your Mission

It almost goes without saying that the most important first step in any process is to have a clear understanding of your objective. In other words, what is your mission? This may seem like an overly-simplistic concept, in that you identify what you want to do and then just go do it, right? For some, perhaps. For others, however, this can be a difficult first step. Sometimes the hardest part of making a change is being able to look inwardly to figure out what you really want to do in life. Some people have many interests and are indecisive about which direction they would like to go. For many, the path to success can take several forms, which can muddy the waters and complicate the decision-making process. It is okay to have multiple or competing interests, but at some point, you have to make a decision. You cannot develop a plan of action based on unclear goals. If you are going to develop a plan to effect the change you seek, you must first be clear about the objective. Keep in mind that you will be speaking to your goals and objectives with different types of people throughout the process. Therefore, you will want to ensure you can clearly articulate what you hope to achieve. If you have multiple interests, separate them so that each one has its own plan of attack. Try to avoid mingling too many goals and objectives, as this will complicate your planning efforts.

If you simply have no idea about what you would like to do, consider taking a personality test, such as the Meyers Briggs Type Indicator Test. This is a widely used personality test that is intended to match your personality and interests to corresponding jobs that align with who you are in terms of personal/professional habits and interests. Most high schools and community colleges offer this personality test. The main limitation of the test is that its accuracy is vitally dependent on the test taker's truthfulness.

For those of you struggling to identify your objective, it may help to prioritize your job criteria. Think about what is most important to you. Is money the most important thing? Do you want to travel? Is it more important to have a healthy work-life balance? My advice is to do something you can be passionate about, regardless of how much money it brings. If you pursue a career field you are not personally driven to do, simply for the money, you will not likely find much happiness in the long run. Once you have prioritized your criteria, you want to start thinking about the types of careers or jobs that meet your objective. Let's say for example that you want to become a fashion editor but are not quite sure how to get there or even

which jobs to pursueto better position yourself for such a career. That's okay. Conducting an informational interview with industry experts will help you flesh out those details, and may even expose unforeseen opportunities along the way.
The most important thing, however, is that you figure out what you want to do. Once you know the end game, you can start developing your milestones.

Set Goals

In keeping with the idea of knowing your objective, setting goals is an integral step in any planning process. Some people tend to gloss over the goal-setting part, insisting that they already know what they want to do. What they fail to realize, however, is that there are usually incremental steps involved with achieving the larger goal. It is a good idea to break down your goals in terms of short and long-term goals. A long-term goal may be the ultimate end-state goal you wish to achieve, such as becoming a fashion editor, journalist, or business owner. Short-term goals are the benchmarks you must accomplish in order to reach that ultimate goal. Accomplishing the short-term goals is the key to accomplishing the larger long-term goal. Keep in mind, you do not win a war in one fell swoop; you win it by executing a series of strategic moves that win battles. People often fall short of their larger goal because the piece they have bitten off is much larger than they can chew at once. You would notjust shove an entire steak into your mouth and swallow it whole. You cut off small pieces and devour it one bite at a time. By establishing short"easily digestible" goals, you gain more and more confidence with each successive goal attained.

If there is one thing I have learned in my personal and professional life, it's that goals must be written down to mean anything. Goals notwritten down are just pipe dreams…wishes. Writing down your goals serves a couple of purposes. First, it makes your goals tangible. Being able to see your goals written down makes them more realistic and allows you to visualize their attainment. Second, written goals that you can look at every day will keep you motivated and help ensure personal accountability. You are less likely to throw in the towel when your goals are right there in your face every day, reminding you of your commitment. I cannot underscore enough the importance of that point. As you develop your goals, be sure to adhere to the S.M.A.R.T. principle. Your goals should be:

Specific: The less general and more specific your goal, the greater your chance of achieving it.

Measurable: Allows you to gauge progress, particularly if several steps are involved.

Attainable: Do you have the capacity to obtain your goal…finances, education, training?

Relevant: Goals should be consistent with your mission or objective.

Time based: The timeframe to achieve them should be specific, not open-ended.

Below is an example of a SMART goal:

Broad Goal: I want to start a jewelry business.

Specific: I will sell homemade jewelry on the Internet.

Measurable: I will be ready to take my first order within four weeks, and I will aim to sell a minimum of five pieces per week.

Attainable: I will establish a website. Then, I will build an inventory of 30 handmade pieces of jewelry to sell. Finally, I will promote my business and build customer relationships through word of mouth, referrals and local networking.

Relevant: Selling homemade jewelry will allow me to benefit financially from my favorite hobby.

Time-Based: My website will be up and running within four weeks, and I will have an inventory of 30 pieces of jewelry within six weeks.

Chapter 15: Researching The Company And Interviewers

Imagine you are heading into a job interview where you know nothing about the company. Can you imagine how such an interview would turn out?

If you don't know much—or even know very little— about the company you intend to work for, you're likely to sit there dumbfounded when interviewers ask you questions such as why you want to work for that business or which role you see yourself playing in it.

When it comes to preparing for a job interview, the first step is to get your hands on as much information as you can about the respective company so you can prepare your answers and pitch accordingly. Here is what you need to do for that.

Extensively Research The Organization/Company

Whenever you apply for a job, it is wise to research the respective company so you know a bit about the company you're applying to work for, its industry, its scope, etc. However, when you are called in for an interview, you need to turn this research into an extensive one. Here is what you need to do:

Extensively research that business/company online and find out as much as you can about its history, work, performance, clients, products/services, any issues it has faced, past and current accomplishments, and net worth, etc. This will help you understand its standing in its respective industry.

For instance, if you're applying for a job in a company that has been in operation for more than 50 years, a company that's constantly growing, you know you are applying to a sound company with good growth opportunities and your motivation to ace your job interview will automatically increase.

The accomplishments give you a better idea of the scope of growth. As for the setbacks, if you know you have a certain skill or talent that can help that organization improve on a weakness that is the cause of a setback, you can add that point to your sales pitch and impress the interviewers.

When researching the working and mode of operation of the company, research its products and services so you know what it deals in and the commodities or services you will be dealing with if you land that job. This helps you brainstorm ideas to improve their goods or tactics to better market them depending on the area/sector of the company you are applying to work in.

While conducting this research, visit the company's website if it has any. Today, most companies or businesses have a website even if it is not a good-looking one. If the organization you applied for does not have a website, tread carefully because it may mean the business or company is not genuine. However, this is not true for all companies: some good companies operate in a local capacity but lack a website. If you cannot find the website, check other online sources for information about the business or company. Read any press releases or articles written on the company. Also check LinkedIn for people related to the company or the company's own profile. LinkedIn is a great social media platform that helps you connect with people from the corporate world. It also has tons of information about organizations.

Find out if the organization you intend to work for has a blog and if it has one, thoroughly scrutinize the information on the company's working, products/services, current or previous promotions and deals, accomplishments, and anything else that can help you create an effective job pitch.

Check the company's Facebook and Twitter accounts—if it has any.

If that company is a public entity, check its SEC filings by visiting sec.gov.

Check out the company's competitors and get as much information as you can about them. This information comes in handy when interviewers ask you questions such as how you can help the company grow or how you can help it become better. You can highlight any strengths of the company's competitors and present your ideas on how you can help this company do even better with your skills and potential.

Make sure you print any important information you discover from your research and place it in a separate file/folder. Go through that information several times until you have a firm understanding of the company/business. When interviewers see you have an in depth knowledge of the company, your homework is likely to impress them to a point where they consider you an ideal candidate for the respective job.

While it is important to research the company you are hoping to work for, it is equally important to know more about your interviewers.

Research Your Interviewers

When a company or business invites you for a job interview, ask about the people who will be interviewing you. Sometimes businesses choose to keep this information to themselves; however, in some cases, the person calling you to schedule an interview will give you the names or designations of your interviewers. Make sure you get both from that person so you can thoroughly research the important people you need to impress on that day.

Knowing more about the interviewers is important because:

It helps you figure out how much effort you need to put into your preparation. Although, you need to prepare to give your best shot in any case, it's natural to become more focused if you know the CEO of the company will be the one interviewing you.

It helps you research the credentials, accomplishments, net worth, and corporate profile of your interviewers. Conducting this research can help you understand what your interviewers will be looking for in the candidates. For instance, if one of your interviewers is a web developer who created a creative approach in the industry or an entrepreneur who has many innovative products to his/her name, you automatically know that the person will be looking for someone with great creativity and the ability to think outside the box. Hence, to impress him/her, your pitch needs to highlight your creative skills.

Research also helps you find information you can identify with and use to convince the interviewer of your idealness for the job. For instance, if a certain interviewer now has a million dollar net worth but started from scratch 6 years ago, you can come up with a pitch that outlines your hard work, resilience, and determination.

You can also find out about the interests, likes and dislikes of your interviewers, and then use that information to captivate their interest. For instance, if you know a certain interviewer is a golf enthusiast, you can talk about the sport (at the right instance) to impress him/her.

Your main goal is to gain a better understanding of your interviewers' backgrounds and professional profile as well as interests so you can establish good rapport. To conduct this research, do the following:

Conduct online research on each person individually

Check individual profiles on Facebook, Twitter, Instagram, LinkedIn, and any other social media platform to find out more about individual likes, dislikes, hobbies, interests, achievements, etc.

Review information about your interviewers on the organization's website

Collect as much information as you can on both the company and the interviewers. Create a softcopy and a hardcopy of the information so you can review it even when you do not have access to the internet or a laptop.

Once you have done your research on the company and the interviewers, the next this is to prepare for commonly asked questions so you can answer them effectively.

Chapter 16: The Interview Basics

In this section, we will discuss the basics of the interview process. We will look into the types of interviews, who you will interview with, the interviewer's strategy, and, of course, the actual interview. From beginning, to end, most hiring structures are as follows:

1. Resume Screening – Screen for potential candidates

2.Phone Interview – More advanced screening process/beginning of the interview phase

3.Interview – Successful screening candidates are called for an interview

4.Second Interview – Successful candidates are called back for a second round. **Note**: Some companies may only have one round, and some may have more than two.

5.Offer Notification – The chosen candidate will receive a phone call and/or email informing them of their decision.

Types of Interviews

Depending on how the company conducts their interviews and what stage you are at in the interview process, there are several different types of interviews. You should find out what type of interview you will be heading into beforehand. Here are several of the most common.

Screening/Phone Interview

Phone interviews are pretty common these days. Phone interviews are conducted after your resume is initially screened and passed. This means that they liked what they saw on paper, but want to get a feel for you on the phone, before they invite you into the office. Typically, a human resources professional will be the one to interview you on the phone. Generally, they will ask you more basic questions and ask you to go over your resume. They want to see that you are personable and well-spoken. The phone interview is crucial to moving on to the next stage and should be taken just as seriously as the in-person interview. After all, if you don't do well during the phone interview chances are good that you won't make it to an actual face-to-face interview.

One-on-One Interview

These are the most common interviews and you'll definitely do them at some point. These interviews consist of just you and the interviewer. They usually take place in a designated area, such as a conference room, office, etc.

Group Interview: Many vs. You

During this type of interview, there will be many members of the hiring group interviewing you at once. This can be anywhere from 2-5 people, sometimes more, depending on the company, industry, position, and so on. During this interview, the "interviewers" will interview you and ask questions. These may seem a bit more difficult at first, but don't worry, you handle this like any other type of interview. Just divvy up your time between the interviewers and try not to neglect anyone.

Group Interview: Many Candidates vs. One Interviewer

When the company is hiring a large number of candidates, they will typically conduct these types of interviews. They will interview several individuals at the same time, often in the same room. This allows the company to compare the answers of each individual directly at that moment. It can seem intimidating for those who are shy, but do not worry; everyone else is in the same position as you. Your preparation will allow you to outshine the other candidates.

Group Interview: Many vs. Many

These types of interviews typically occur in the beginning stages of the hiring process. There will be many candidates in a room, together with many employees of the company. They will give you a background on the company, the position, and what is on the agenda for the rest of the interview. You will typically break out into a one vs. one interview after. These types of interviews are done to save the company time.

Who You'll Meet

As mentioned, you will most likely be interviewing with several different types of people. It's important to recognize who they are prior to the interview, since questions should be tailored to each.

Human Resources/Recruiter

In most interviews, you will first be interviewing with the human resources representative designated for hiring and filling your position. Most likely, you have already had some interaction with this person before. They are the individual who initially screened your resume and asked you to come in for an interview. They felt your qualifications were impressive enough and feel you are a potential fit for the open position.

The important thing to note with the human resources interviewer is that he/she is looking for a "general fit," for both the position and the company. The interviewer most likely had conversations with the hiring manager and roughly knows the qualifications desired for the position. They are also well aware of the culture and atmosphere of their company, so they want to see whether you would fit in well. They will most likely ask you general-type questions. Here is your opportunity to show your interest in the company, as well as show that you are personable.

Members of the Group

More than likely, you will be interviewing with different members of the group in which the open position is located. It's possible to meet with only 1 or 2, but in a large company or for large teams you may meet with 8 or more members. It is critical that you are able to connect with these individuals. They are the people who you are going to be working with on a daily basis. They want to know you are a person who they can get along with and spend 40 hours a week together. Try to find out their interests and relate to them.

Group Leader

While human resources and members of the group are both extremely important interviews, the group leader will be the person who has the most clout regarding the decision. He/She will be asking you specific questions about your ability to perform the responsibilities related to the position. You need to convey to this person that you are more than capable for the position. They want to see that you will be an overall positive contribution to the group and fulfill their needs. For that reason, you'll want to relate to this person. If you can get them to like you, it will be a major influence come decision-making time.

With this being said, keep in mind that every interview is equally important. You should not slack off or take one less seriously than the other. Once the interview is finished, all interviewers get together and collaborate on what they thought of each candidate. If you rub one person the wrong way, it's just that easy to cross you off the list.

Their Strategy

Interviewers, especially seasoned ones, have a strategy for conducting interviews. They use certain tactics for revealing valuable information from candidates. They have spent countless hours discovering and fine-tuning these methods over the years, and it is kind of their secret to revealing hidden information.

> **Pants Down Tip**
> Understanding the reason behind the interviewer asking the question will help you to answer it properly and not be caught with your pants down

Open-Ended Questions

Nearly all interviewers will ask you open-ended questions. An open-ended question is simply a question that requires more than a yes/no answer. They will ask you something vague and expect you to go with it. These will seem annoying, especially if you are not prepared for them.

Example:

Interviewer: How would you describe yourself?

The interviewer wants to see how you respond to this open-ended question. Basically, they are giving you a little bit and asking you to take it from there. These types of questions allow the interviewer to get to know you better. Describe your very best qualities and always steer the question towards the positives. However, make sure that you aren't being too vague with your responses or giving one word answers.

Penetration Questions

The interviewer knows what they want to get out of you beforehand. He/She also knows that the best method for gaining the information they want is to lead up to it. They do this by asking a series of questions on a particular topic, starting from a very broad perspective and gradually increasing in detail. By the time they are finished, you will have revealed a whole lot more about the topic than if they had simply asked one broad, all-encompassing question. Let's take a look at an example.

Example:

Interviewer: What were your thoughts on your last position?

Interviewer: Did you enjoy the work?

Interviewer: What was the thing you most enjoyed about it?

Interviewer: What was the thing you least enjoyed about it?

Interviewer: Did you have any issues with the company while you were there?

Interviewer: Why did you decide to leave?

As you can see, the interviewer leads with several questions prior to asking why you left your past position. This reveals more about your time at the last company, whether you enjoyed or disliked it, but also lays down a foundation for some possible reasons that you might have left. The interviewer gets MUCH more information out of you than straight up asking why you left.

Moments of Silence

Interviewers will often use this strategy to get more out of you, to see you further expound on your answer, and/or to see what you might have to say. If the interviewer just asked you a question and you responded, but they are still silent when you thought you were finished answering, think again. They are expecting more of a response, so keep going with it. The interviewer may also be expecting you to ask questions about the subject you're discussing without directly asking you. Your ability to read the interviewer's body language is valuable in this situation.

Hint: Take the interviewers silence as your signal to speak!

Repeated Questions

If the interviewer is looking for more information about a particular topic of interest, they will start using repetition tactics in order to extract more information. These may seem a bit annoying and pushy, but it allows the interviewer to see how well you can back up what you've said and provides them with greater detail on the subject.

Example:

You: I analyzed data by creating complex spreadsheets in Excel.

Interviewer: Complex spreadsheets?

You: Yes. I would create pivot tables in order to better summarize the data.

Interviewer: Pivot tables?

You: Yes, the Excel tool used to summarize data. It allows you to count, sort, total, and average, along with many other functions within a spreadsheet. I learned how to use this tool during my college mathematics course. It's really useful.

See how the interviewer is repeating back what you said? They want to see exactly what you mean by certain phrases and this is one of their strategies for seeing how knowledgeable you are about something.

Yes, they might know what a pivot table is, but they want to see if YOU really know. If you aren't sure about the material you're discussing, penetration questions are sure to catch you with your pants down. This is why it is so important not to claim anything you can't back up.

Comparison Questions

This method is used in order to obtain more information about a particular topic they are interested in and to see how well you're able to relate to topics. They might be wondering how you feel about something or what you learned from it. This also allows the interviewer to see how well you connect different areas of your various experiences and expertise.

Example:

Interviewer: How do you feel your studies in college relate to your job responsibilities?

In this example, the interviewer is looking to see how you compare and contrast your experiences in college with the duties of the prospective job if offered. They want to see how you can connect the two and take away advantages of each, but they also want to see that you are able to differentiate between the two. This shows the interviewer that you're able to see connections. Literally everything has some sort of connection, and a valuable employee is able to see and understand these.

"What if" Scenarios

Hypothetical questions allow the interviewer to see how you would deal with certain situations. These are asked in order to see how you think and the different ways you would go about solving the "problem." They will typically make up a certain scenario using pieces from actual case studies and see you answer it.

Example:

Interviewer: It's 6:00 P.M. on a Wednesday evening and you have a project due at 8:00 AM the next day. Management is using this project to present to clients, so it is extremely important. You've finished the project and are ready to print it but the one printer in the office is down. The IT department has left for the day and you have no expertise when it comes to printers. What are your next steps?

The interviewer is giving you a hypothetical scenario that imposes a tremendous amount of stress on you. They want to see your thought processes regarding breaking down the problem in a reasonable manner. I'll repeat myself; they want to see your THOUGHT PROCESS. The final solution is less important than how you arrive at it for these types of questions.

Chapter 17: The Whirlpool Tool

Put yourself in a belief that if you are attending a fifteen minutes interview, every minute of those fifteen minutes presents an equal opportunity for you to showcase your capabilities. I have heard this bullshit myth circulating around from a long time "Your selection or rejection is decided in the first thirty seconds of your interview and rest of the interview is just a justification" bullshit. Absolute bullshit. A recruiter is not omniscient nor does he possesses any superhuman powers to do so.

Please know that interview is a process a recruiter has to uncover certain dimensions of your personality to select or reject you. Do not forget you need to demonstrate your willingness, ability and suitability for the job. As long as you don't fail to do so a recruiter will not reject you.

I still remember one guy came for interview. He seemed to be in a lot of panic as droplets of sweat were visible on his forehead. The first thing he said was "I am sorry I will not be able to attend this interview as I lost my cell phone just sometime back. I had just got it delivered in the morning and I still could not set up the security password as I was in a hurry. My entire social identity including my Gmail account, Facebook account, watsapp etc. is at stake. Will you mind rescheduling this interview?" What do you expect the recruiter to tell? Obviously "please look into your email to find the revised schedule" where did the 30 seconds bullshit myth go? If you go by the myth what you will find is an extremely panicked candidate who lacks maturity.

Now this doesn't mean that the first thirty seconds don't matter nor does it mean that these are not the most critical thirty seconds. All I mean to say is that the first thirty seconds of your interview do cast a shadow on the rest of your interview but then every next minute provides you an opportunity or a threat to make it or break it. So if you are believe you did a wonderful job in the first thirty seconds, continue it. If you think you were pathetic in the first thirty seconds no worries. You still have fourteen and a half minutes.

I have observed this on multiple occasions that candidates often end up under-delivering in an interview because they are unable to answer the first or the first few questions. This is because of the lack of confidence and loss of motivation carries itself forward to the next question. I have often felt that a candidate's performance at an interview is highly impacted by those minutes of the interview that have already elapsed adversely affecting the remaining minutes.

Please understand you cannot reverse the arrow of time and get those minutes back though you can certainly assure that you don't allow those to adversely affect the rest of your interview.

This motivated me to think of some sort of a mechanism that could allow a candidate to be equally motivated and excited about every question irrespective of how good/bad the candidate was in the preceding questions. In other words some sort of a refreshing system that could refresh the candidate after every question. Think why windows provides a refresh tool across all its versions? It is obviously to terminate those processes which are not in active use but are slowing down the system resulting in an instant increase in the system performance.

Considering all this, what I found the candidates might need is an imaginary whirlpool that works like a refresh tool in an interview that pulls in or suckles all the odd moments resulting in an instant boost in confidence.

I will elaborate

I want you to imagine a whirlpool somewhere in the interview room. Preferably on the ground. Any question that you are unable to handle well should go straight to the whirlpool. This will allow you not to loose confidence to face the remaining interview and to be refreshed.

Imagine you are in an interview.

The first question you are asked is "Mr …………………… tell me something about yourself" you are fully prepared and preparedness synthesizes confidence. You start in a natural tone "Hi my name is ………………….." and then another recruiter throws the second question on you, a tough one "Mr. ……………………… do you consider yourself successful? Your grades have been poor throughout academics and you do not seem to be very actively involved in any co-curricular activities either" you are struck you don't have an answer. No worries. All you have to do is to allow the question to go straight to the whirlpool. Remember the second question has gone and you cannot allow it spoil the next question. Sadly this is what happens more often than not.

So to stay equally energized and enthusiastic throughout the interview, do use the whirlpool tool when needed.

Chapter 18: What Is A Job And Why Do We Want It?

The idea of doing a job is to work for someone and gain something in return. The purpose of doing it is to survive in the economic rat race. A job is nothing but a work that a person does expecting to gain something from it.

When corporate fever had not taken over the world, jobs used to works people used to enjoy doing without expecting anything back, except for mental satisfaction and smiles. However today, with the great economic depression wrecking chaos on the economic cycle across the globe, a job has turned into more precious a thing than life itself.

What is the point of hunting a job? The answer isn't simple and comes in a series of points, some of which have been discussed below.

A job is supposed to burn your kitchen gas. Without a livelihood, a man cannot even dream to sustain his household. It keeps the kitchen fires burning and his diesel cars running. Money, amongst other things, is the ultimate purpose of hunting for a job.

Sustenance is the primary aim of every creature that roams the earth. With so heavily economized a world, it has come down to currency to help man survive. Man, being the smartest animal alive has taken resort to looking for jobs instead of creating one in desperation.

A person's social position is largely determined by what he is worthy of. Besides his values, his job and its pay package decides his social worth. Despite how narrow it sounds, people look at his purse string while deciding how socially upward or otherwise he is.

A job necessarily doesn't have to be all about survival and economic gains. Sometimes, people do enjoy what they work on. However, most times that's not the case. Regardless, mental satisfaction remains in the race of being the priorities of a job hunting person.

It has become extremely difficult to enjoy what you work on and work on what you enjoy. You may have a law degree but you may not get a good job in a law firm. If a group of chartered accounts hires you, you are not likely to refuse the job only because you have to do something in order to start earning.

Besides food, shelter and cloth, job has become one of the main pillars of human survival. Look around and you will find everyone being engaged in their own jobs. These jobs may range from being a mason to chairing a mega company.

Despite how small the job is, the engagement is constant. Everyone is working tirelessly to survive in this cruel world. But is it that easy to land a job of your dreams? Let's find out in the next chapter.

Chapter 19: The Interview Mindset

This chapter will serve as the foundation upon which the subsequent chapters are built. While most books dedicate hundreds of pages to the practical tips in the last few chapters, they will serve no purpose if not accompanied with the interview mindset.

Why is the interview mindset so important? Simply because we live out who we believe we are. We act out our self-given identity. And if you don't see yourself as the most competent person that should be hired, there is no way you will act the part.

So what is the interview mindset? It is simply the mindset that seeks nothing from people and only for people.

Let me explain.

It is only when you don't seek anything from people, be it their attention, their adoration, their acceptance. It's only when you don't need that will you even have a chance of earning it. People are repelled by neediness, perhaps because they see themselves in it. But when they come across somebody who is confident, secure, and not needing of people's adoration, people begin to notice.

And then to seal the deal, when this confident person is not only self-sufficient, but seeks the good of others, people cannot help but be drawn in. Why? Because this is counterintuitive. It's not normal. But when you learn how to master this mindset, you learn how to win people.

The reality is, people like, trust, hire, and follow people that:

They like and admire

Like and are interested in them

Are similar to them

We're going to break this mindset into five principles or the five pillars that create this mindset.

It is crucial that you develop these mental habits overtime to master life's interviews.

Principle #1: Be the Leader

Be the leader. Even when you're not. Display authority, even when you don't have it. The truth is, you don't need an actual position of leadership to give off a sense of influence. Not at all. Leadership happens when you come across as somebody who knows what he or she's doing. Somebody with an established sense of self and purpose.

In the interview room, this looks like you displaying confidence in yourself. It means walking into the interview with the mindset that your time is limited and valuable, you have other options (or will have them), you know that this company desperately needs to fill this position, and you'll give them some time to sell it to you.

What you enter the room with that mindset, your responses and your attitude will inevitably change. It will be completely different than walking into the room, fingers-crossed, palms sweaty, hoping they'll like you and your resume out of the other 200 applicants.

No.

The first step is to tell yourself that you do not need this job. You'll find other jobs. You'll find other ways. But your life does not depend on this job, this interview, or this hiring manager. You refuse to give them that power over you.

A CEO or military general will never walk into a conference room, hoping the conversation will go well and people will like them. They have too many other things to care about and their time is limited. Their existence, security, reputation, or self-worth simply is not be threatened by anybody in that room and everybody knows that when they walk in.

At this point you might argue: But they already have a job. They already have respect. They are already in that position of leadership so of course it's easy for them.

And that's where you're wrong. Because successful CEO's, generals, and leaders all had this mindset long before they ever got their position. In fact, it was this very mindset that got them there.

All this to say that you must wake up every morning with a clear sense of who you are and what your purpose is. If you don't know what it is, then find it. Write it out on paper. You need to know your mission in this world and your unique contribution that only YOU can offer. Not Bill Gates, not Steve Jobs, not your hiring manager, not your next-door neighbor, but you. What skill, personality trait, talent, or experience that you uniquely have that sets you apart. And then ask yourself this question: With my uniqueness, what difference in this world am I called to make?

It could be that you have a keen eye for imagining designs and ideas that have yet to be created, that the world needs.

It could be that you're a great organizer and you're called to lead groups of people to new endeavors.

Whatever it is, don't do anything until you answer this question.

When you answer this question and give your life to it, leadership begins. When you have embraced this mindset, you'll be able to walk into any room as a leader with a defined mission and defined personal values. A mission and values that you believe with complete conviction are necessary and beneficial for this world and for everybody in it. That includes your hiring manager, when you walk in for your interview.

And when you've fully embraced this vision of yourself and of your life, you will start to become somebody who doesn't need anything from others, at all. And that's the beginning of leadership.

"The question isn't who is going to let me; it's who is going to stop me." Ayn Rand.

Principle #2: Be Knowledgeable

To be a true leader and true master of interviews and life, you must be knowledgeable. There is no way around this. You must commit yourself to a lifelong quest of learning and growing in your knowledge.

You can tell immediately who the leader in the room is by seeing who everybody naturally turns to when a question is asked. Even if they don't have the official position of authority. Why? Because they're the most likely to know the answer. And those who know are those we follow.

Every great leader in history has been a reader of books, journals, magazines, and nowadays, blogs and web articles. It is only through a cultivated habit of learning that you begin to get a grasp on how everything connects in this world, from economics, to political science, to stock market, to human psychology, biology, and even chemistry.

This isn't to say that you need to be an expert on every subject. That would be impossible and a futile endeavor. Yet to at least have a framework on these different arenas and sectors of life and society is to grant you access to the top 10% of people who stand out above the crowd. The 10% of people who are likely to be followed.

There is a reason for this.

The sad reality is too often our educational systems are flawed in that we are encouraged to pursue academics over education. We are rewarded for our test-taking skills, rather than our skill of creativity and success.

Most of society is trained to live by the system and to strive for the things the system encourages: Get straight A's, study for long hours to pass exams (even if you don't grasp the material), partake in activities purely to buff up your resume, go to college and get a degree, study for the sake of studying and passing, get an internship position or two, and then start applying for jobs. Hopefully you land a job and you can settle into a comfortable life.

This creates a societal tunnel-vision. We have sacrificed education for systematic academics that are only rewarded if we follow the system and pattern that has been laid out for us.

This type of learning does not create leaders.

True leaders move beyond that, whether intentionally or unintentionally, and seek to learn how the world works. They seek to learn how people work and how culture works.

This happens through education, not academics. This happens through personal study driven by passion, not punishment. This is motivated by curiosity, not curriculums.

And if you develop and master this habit of constantly learning not for the sake of grades, but for the sake of growth, then you will have a break through. Not many people make it through this. Too many are content with playing the academic game, doing whatever it takes to get good grades, to get good resumes, to get mediocre jobs, and submit themselves to whatever the system, hiring managers, and organizations want from them, for the rest of their lives.

You must break free from this.

It is when you develop this habit, you will be a leader and be somebody worth following. You will seek to create, not simply to conform. You will be defined by a passion to sail the seas, rather than the fear of rocking the proverbial boat.

When you master these two principles we've talked about so far, you will become a person that people esteem; that people like; that people admire. That is the first step to leadership and that is the first step to the interview mindset.

Principle #3: Be an Expert Affirmer

The natural disposition of a person is to live a self-absorbed life. It's a sad reality, but as I mentioned in the first few pages of this book, that's how I lived.

As human beings, we are all naturally self-centered and overly self-conscious. Call it psychology, or evolutionary traits, or sin, or whatever worldview you come from, we cannot deny this fact. But we can use it to our advantage.

Remember, the three types of people that people like?

People that they like

People that like them

People that are like them.

The first two principles (be a leader and be knowledge) set you up to be the first type of person. People like leaders. People follow those that are not needy or dependent on others. And people admire those that are knowledgeable.

To be the second type of person is the goal of this principle.

If you want somebody to like you and trust you, you must be their biggest affirmer. You must be their biggest fan. You must exhibit genuine curiosity in their life, their hobbies, their passions, their struggles, and their fears. You must authentically want to know more about them and they will know if you are authentic or not.

And the only way to genuinely show border-line obsessive interest in somebody is to be a person that does not need anything from them. In other words: **get over yourself**. You simply cannot be genuinely interested in their life if you are desperately dependant and in need of their approval or affirmation.

You must resolve firmly that you do NOT need this person to like you, whether it's a girl or boy you're romantically interested in, or if it's a hiring manager, or a new classmate. You must find this sense of self-approval elsewhere. You must be self-secured in your own sense of self-worth, in your values, and in your unique mission.

Then, and only then, can you devote yourself to being interested in other people. And believe me, these type of people are rare. But I'm sure you know that.

Let's bring this back to the interview room.

If you walk in to the interview room, not nervous about getting this job because you don't need this job. Not wringing your hands, nervously hoping you'll be accepted. Instead, if you walk in, confident in your purpose, with the mindset that you are giving them the opportunity to hire you, you are freed to act naturally. You will be more relaxed and be an expert affirmer. Your job now is to do your best to naturally affirm whatever you can about them, making them feel valuable and liked. They will remember this.

Whenever you have conversations with new people, who are the people you remember to this day? People that complimented you. People that said nice things about you and affirmed you. Even if it was as simple as them saying they liked your shoes or your shirt. Do you remember how you immediately felt about those people? You liked them.

If you were a hiring manager, conducting hundreds of interviews with hundreds of people a day, who would you remember?

Those that made you feel affirmed and special.

You can comment on how you like their shirt, or if the topic arises, you can casually start a conversation about their hobbies or their life. Only people with this right mindset can ever hope to accomplish this naturally, and it's these people that get hired to become leaders.

Principle #4: Get in Their World

This principle deals with the last type of person that people like: People that are like them. If you've ever been a new place, whether traveling, or a new school, or a new job, who do you gravitate towards?

People that are like you.

It could be anything from how they dress, their ethnicity, their personality, etc. And when you start to get to know people more, you're drawn even closer to those who share similar interests as you, whether hobbies, or religion, or past experiences.

Those with the interview mindset know this well and will do everything to make these connections. When these connections are made, hiring managers are 50% more likely to remember your name.

Obviously you're going to want to do this naturally. In other words, this does not call for an awkward, "Hi I'm Henry, WHAT DO YOU LIKE TO DO?" Experts at this try to naturally thread this into a conversation.

"You've got an interesting last name. May I ask where it's from?"

And since everybody loves taking about themselves, they'll answer. At this point, you can say:

"Oh, it's French? I went to France 2 years ago, it was beautiful!"

Or if you didn't go to France,

"Oh that's lovely! I have a friend from France and she's always raving about

If you're lucky, this might spark further conversation. You might not be able to make connections easily, but this is a skill you must develop. You must train your eyes to look for things that could create conversations.

What does their coffee mug say?

What does their University Diploma say? What did they study?

What does their tattoo mean?

If you can establish a connection with them (or anybody in life), this will put you in a different league all together. You'll realize that this skill will be directly increased by how skilled you are in principle 2.

Principle #5: Be Reserved

This fifth and last principle might seem a bit out of place, but there is a good reason for this component of this mindset. Bluntly stated, people admire those who never show all of their cards. I don't mean in a shady, suspicious kind of way causing people to question whether or not you're a murderer.

Rather, I mean to suggest to act in such a way that you always have things under control, even when you don't. Always appear to have an alternative plan, for the sake of others. Why? Because people look to leaders who have answers, even when the leaders don't have answer.

This is a common human characteristic and it's often exhibited in the movies we watch. All of the leaders that are portrayed as respected are also portrayed as slightly mysterious and reserved, as if they always know something we don't and we can trust them for that. Just a few examples of this are Dumbledore, Professor Xavier, Yoda, Batman, Jack Sparrow, Jesus, Rick Grimes (Walking Dead), Oliver Queen (Arrow). We can go on forever.

Take note that it's not that we are borrowing from the movies and fantasy. Instead, it's the reserve. The movies simply portray the characteristics of human nature. We look up to leaders that seem to always know what they're doing and are reserved and humble about it.

Chapter 20: Getting Started

I cannot stress enough how important preparing for a job interview is! Keep in mind that you only get one chance to show your potential to the prospect employer and why you are the best applicant for the position. Sadly, there are a lot of qualified candidates who fail to spend the time to prepare themselves for the interviews and successively miss out on the offer they want.

Requesting for Interview

Requesting for a job interview may sound like a simple and easy thing to do that writing about it seem unnecessary. Although I'd agree in a way, there seemed to be some candidates who manage to start out on the wrong way when they do this. Whether the outcome is good or bad, it is always the first impression that you're giving to the interviewer is one of the most important things to take into consideration. So, below is the best way how you can schedule or set a job interview:

Phone Call Interview

Before the face-to-face interviews, the employer or the HR should be aware that you are coming, and one of the best ways to inform them is through a telephone call. Here are important tips to guarantee a successful telephone call with an interviewee:

- Call during a time when you wouldn't get distracted.
- If possible, use a landline to make a call.
- Take control of your surroundings. Make sure that your dog is not chained and not going to bark during the call. Make sure your baby is asleep and someone's going to take care of her when she cries. Make sure the TV is off and your mobile phone on silent.
- Have a glass of water at reach so when your mouth gets dry
- Have a pen and paper at hand so you can write anything you need to take note of during the phone call.

- Talk clearly and slow enough for the person at the other end to understand every word you say.
- Don't multitask. Pay close attention to the process. You don't want to make the interviewer repeat what they said as they'll think that you're not being attentive.

Walk-in Interview

A walk-in interview is a job interview that takes place without having an appointment. They're common at job fairs, bur many business establishments allow it. This meeting tends to be fairly short and usually made up of only quite a few questions. At the end of the interview, the employer may or may not tell you whether you are hired or not. However, most of the time, walk-in interviews are only used to narrow down the list of people who have might be perfect for the job. The chosen candidates are normally invited for a new formal meeting at a later date.

The Setting

A walk-in interview is meant to be unplanned and spontaneous. However, you can still follow some structures in order to make sure nothing will go wrong. There is where we called a job fair where employers get the opportunity to meet hundreds of job applicants interested in working for them at once. Job interviews that take place at these kinds of events normally occur at an open-air booth or in a private conference room, usually not far from the employer's office.

There are companies that also host walk-in interview events right at their offices every time there are many vacant positions that need to be filled right away. Anyone who is wanted to work at the company is normally allowed to go to the events and be interviewed without much stress or hassle.

Getting Ready

The good thing about with this kind of meetings is that the applicant looks more casual than they actually are in the eyes of the employer. Although most are intended to be informal, it's best to be prepared when going to a walk-in interview. The preparation should be the same as if you are going on a scheduled job interview.

It's normally a great idea for applicants to wear a formal outfit and be ready with a list of references and some copies of your previous resumes. Applicants who look elegant and professional, even in a spontaneous meeting, are normally the best placed to create a good impression that can ultimately land a job that you want.

Preparing Resume

A good resume is difficult to find. It's important to put a lot of thought and effort on making them and for a lot of candidates, help from the professional might be necessary.

A good resume has developed and changed throughout the last decades. There are different styles of formatting and writing used prospective applicants. However, you have to keep in mind that a good resume cannot guarantee you landing the job, but it will give you an advantage.

If you want to find an effective technique for a job interview, the one that will set you apart from the other applicants is the way you presented your resume. There are many ways to make sure that your resume is better than other applicants.

There are many companies that are dedicated to generating the best quality resumes possible and could help you land the job you want. Below are some of the most important things you must know when you submit your resume:

Tips for Making a Good Resume

Knowing the important tips when making a resume is very important. There are a lot of job hunters fail to get their jobs because of how they present their resume. You have to keep in mind that even before you get interviewed your employer is a lot likely look at your resume first before he even talks to you. Here are important things to remember when creating your resume.

Make Sure Your Previous Experience is Relevant

If you're applying for an office job, chances are your potential employer doesn't care if you worked at McDonald's when you are 17. One great mistake a lot of people make is getting confused on what past jobs you need to include in your resume. Yes, you're asked to list down the job history, but it's important to include only the relevant ones.

Don't Use the Contact Information of Your Current Employer

It is astounding how many people include the contact information of their current employer in their resume. This is a huge mistake. First of all, if you have others calling you on your current job, then that's considered as time-theft and can be called for notice. Secondly, it will reflect badly on your potential employer who will think that you might do the same.

Get a Painstaking Guide and Follow It

Don't simply sit down and put up your resume the way you always did. Don't simply open up an MS Word and randomly throw around work experience, write sub-headings and bulleted list. You have to research what's the best thing to add to your resume and essentially apply the techniques that work best to your resume. You'll be amazed at how following small, small tips can make a drastic improvement on your application.

Making a Follow-up

A lot of people getting interviewed for a position do not take the time to make a follow-up. They assume that the employer might be busy or they didn't want to look so desperate for the job so they just wait for them to call. In several cases, following up does not necessary as you might not like the job being offered after learning more about them during the interview.

Regardless of how you feel about the interview, you have to remember that following up doesn't mean desperation, instead of enthusiasm, and this is what many employers want in their applicants. However, there's a wrong and right way to follow up your job interview.

So, how would you follow-up your job interview the right way?

First of all, you will want to consider follow-up as a part of your job hunt tactic. Think of it as a valuable tool to get the job that you want. Although you must focus more on the interview itself, make sure that you leave all the important information at the end of the interview. You can take some notes while on the interview which you can use as your reference for the follow-up.

Don't forget to ask how the hiring process works and when you might get notified if ever you get the job, you must not also forget the name and the positions of the persons involved in your job interview. Furthermore, make sure that you have the contact information of those who interviewed you for the follow-up.

Whichever method you prefer, whether it is email or text, make sure to show gratitude to the interviewer by thanking them in the message. With a simple thank-you email or letter to everyone who took their time to get to know your qualification for the job, you're giving them more reason as to why they should hire you.

Before mailing or emailing your notes check them carefully for grammar and spelling. If your message includes an intention to follow up by phone, in the future, be sure to add that call to your calendar prior to sending.

Making the Actual Follow Up

It is true that most of the time, the employer or the hiring manager can be busy. They cannot dedicate all their time to answer calls from the job applicants. However, don't be afraid to attempt a call even only once. Do it one week after the interview.

Follow up can be tricky. You do not want to end up being annoying and at the same time, you don't want to miss the opportunity you may have if you only call them. The secret is to know when and how you should do it.

Chapter 21: Interview Do's And Don'ts

If you want to increase your chances of obtaining the job for which you are applying, you need to know what is acceptable and what is not when you go for an interview. However, these may seem like small things, but doing the right things can make the difference in your potential for being hired. It is important to know what things may earn you extra points and those that will take away and cost you the opportunity for that job. Although most people know the basic things to do and not do during an interview, those who are looking for their first job—at least their first full-time job—may not be aware of those things.

Things to do before and during an interview
- Find out something about the company
- Be ready with your printed resume
- Make sure you have proper clothing for an interview (professional or business casual depending on the company)

- Prepare a list of questions you want to ask the interviewer(s)
- Have a notebook and pen to take notes during the interview
- Be 10 minutes early for the interview—if there are circumstances beyond your control call the interviewer and give him or her the option to still see you or reschedule the interview
- Turn your mobile phone alert on vibrate or off during the interview
- Send a Thank You note to the interviewer as soon as possible after the interview. This increases your chances of being hired.

Things not to do before or during the interview

- Do not schedule interviews too close together in case there are additional things you need to do such tests or traffic
- Do not bring your children or anyone else with you to an interview unless they are also applying for a position
- Never smoke during an interview even if you are allowed to do so
- Never snack or chew gum. Finish your

snack before the interview or throw away your gum before the interview. Bring a mouth spray will be advised
- Stay on topic during the interview and avoid personal discussions
- Do not bring drinks into the interview—if the interviewer asks if you would like coffee, tea or water you may then accept.

Choose Your Words Wisely

Many people lose good opportunities because they fail to use professional and grammatically correct language during an interview. If you do not use correct grammar in your daily life, you will need to use it during a job interview. It may seem perfectly fine to use double negatives and slang when you are dealing with friends and co-workers, but if you want to win positive points during an interview, you have to speak as though you are educated. During an interview never under any circumstances, use slang or curse words. For some, that might mean thinking carefully before speaking but it is a very important if you hope to find a job or to find a new one. What is acceptable at your current office or at home is not acceptable in an interview. Your choice of words can make a difference in whether you are chosen for the job for which you applied. If you feel you are not confident in your grammar skills, take a some time to brush up on some common word choices before you go to the interview

The topic of your conversation is another area where you need to be very professional during an interview. Even if you know the interviewer personally, you should not use the interview to share jokes or events outside the topic of the interview. There is a time for personal discussions and the job interview is not one of them. Choose your words carefully, make sure they are related to the interview and that you present yourself as a professional rather than someone who is in need of further education. Avoid attempting to use big words whose meaning you do not know just to make yourself look more intelligent than you are—if you use a word in the wrong context you will make yourself appear desperate to overcompensate in the eyes of the interviewer and will probably cost you the position for which you are applying.

Multiple Requests: Choosing The Best Options

What do you do when you send out many resumes and get multiple requests for interviews? If you are unemployed time is not a problem but what happens when you are searching for a career change and only have a limited amount of time for interviews? How do you choose from among all the requests? One of the best things to do is choose those that are closest to what you are seeking. When you have a limited amount of time it's important to choose those interviews that would benefit your career most.

If you have several possibilities that might be good career choices, you may need to weigh all of the possibilities including taking a few hours off from your current position in order to go for the interviews that are most interesting to you. If you restrict yourself to a certain number of interviews, you may have difficulty finding the position you really want. That doesn't mean you should take a lot of time off your current job to go to all interview for many different positions. However, you want to be able to schedule your time so that you can fit in all of the interviews that you like the most. Avoid accepting requests for interviews that do not directly promote your choice of a career.

Once you are able to manage your schedule to fit the interviews for the positions that best meet your career objectives, you need to make sure you follow proper interview protocol to increase your chances for being hired. That means you want to dress appropriately and have a proper discussion in the interview. By narrowing your choices of interviews to take, you will be able to manage everything without interfering with your current working hours or duties. Be selective yet look to the best career choices at the same time in order to diminish your interview time.

Chapter 22: Analyze Your Strengths, Weaknesses, Opportunities, And Threats

A lot of people have the misconception that a SWOT (strengths, weaknesses, opportunities, and threats) analysis is only useful to companies and organization. Actually, it is also applicable to job seekers as well.

If you have career goals, you can definitely use the SWOT analysis to further understand yourself and your competitors. You have to determine your strengths and weaknesses. On the other hand, you also have to know your external opportunities and threats. You have to see yourself as a product and your career as your business.

Know Your Strengths

If you understand yourself, you're able to put yourself in the market easily. Your strengths are your asset and can be a differentiating feature of yourself from your competitors. Your interviewer may ask you questions about your strengths so you have to know them. Your strengths may include proven sales abilities, ability to present to large audiences, proven expertise in reengineering processes, or solid project management skills.

Understand Your Weaknesses

A personal weakness may be treated as an opportunity or a liability. It is a characteristic which you can improve on so that you'll have more job opportunities. Your weaknesses may include poor listener, tendency to procrastinate, fear of speaking to large groups, or disorganization.

Be Objective About Opportunities And Threats

If you consider your opportunities and threats, you have to compare yourself with your competitors for the next job promotion or career. You have to carefully study these people so that you can find every possible way to better compete with them. An example of a threat is other job seekers who have higher educational attainment than you. An opportunity is for you to study again at night so that you can attain higher learning. A threat may be your colleague who is confident in presenting to large groups. An opportunity is for you to join a program or take a speech class.

The personal SWOT analysis is for you to identify the possible actions you can take to move up the career ladder or get the job that you want. If you compare your strengths and weaknesses to the requirements of the job, you can better prepare yourself for the job interview.

Creating The Personal SWOT Analysis

Strengths

You have to include all your internal positive aspects which you can capitalize on and control like your work experience; educational attainment; technical knowledge; transferable skills like leadership skills, teamwork, communication; and personal characteristics.

Weaknesses

You can think about all internal negative aspects which you can improve on and control like limited education; lack of work experience; lack of goals; weak leadership, communication, interpersonal, and teamwork skills; negative personal characteristics; and weak job-hunting skills.

Opportunities

You have to consider all positive external conditions which you can take advantage of even if you can't control them. In addition, you can also include all positive trends within your field of expertise which you believe will create more jobs. Opportunities you can have if you enhance your education, self-knowledge, job goals, and professional develop are also a must.

Threats

Threats are negative external conditions which you can't control but can reduce the impact. These can also be negative trends within your field which can reduce jobs. You can also include competitors with better knowledge, experience, skills, and job-hunting skills.

Sample Interview Questions And Answers

Question: What important characteristics do you have?

Why this may be asked: The interviewer wants to know how your strengths can help you with the job he's offering.

Possible answer: You can reply with your personal characteristics like determination, good analytical skills, persistence, etc. You can say, "I'm assertive and very confident" or "I have good communication skills."

You can expound by saying that "I am confident and assertive. I try to understand the problems of customers so I can solve them. This way, these customers can remain loyal to the company."

"My exemplary communication skills were able to help me handle company workshops and presentations with confidence. I can easily impart my views with large groups of people."

"My two years experience in customer service has helped me hone my customer relations and customer service skills."

Question: What are your negative characteristics?

Why this may be asked: The job interviewer wants to know if you're aware of your flaws and how these may affect your work performance.

Possible answer: Although it is difficult to share your negative traits with a job interviewer, it is a good idea to be more diplomatic. You can't say something which can have an effect with how you can perform the job you're applying for. In addition, you can't say "I don't have any negative traits." You have to let your interview know that you are aware of your negative characteristics and you're confident that these won't, in any way, affect how you do your job.

You can say, "Sometimes, I get to be very much involved with the tiny details so execution is delayed."

"It's very difficult for me to say 'No" to anyone asking for help."

You can't highlight your negative traits. You have to give diplomatic answers which can highlight your strengths. You can also talk about improving yourself as you work on the job. Keep your answers direct to the point so you don't give your interviewer some unnecessary insights about yourself.

Question: Can you work under a lesser-experienced superior?

Why this may be asked: The interviewer wants to know how you deal with unexpected events in the workplace.

Possible answer: You can answer him by saying, "Working with that superior may cause some conflict but it will also provide me with an opportunity to work on my teamwork skills so I can handle conflicts better."

Question: How do you handle things in the office which you can't control?

Why this may be asked: The interviewer wants to find out how you handle threats in the workplace.

Possible answer: You can say, "I try to minimize the effects of competition in the office by acquiring training on some particular skills that I lack."

"I try to avoid overworking myself by employing some time management strategies."

"I cope up with the requirements of the job by upgrading my proficiencies and skills in order to keep abreast with changes in the workplace and in the industry."

Resumes

Like cover letters, resumes need to be neat, clean, and to the point. They are simply a precise, measurable timeline of your accomplishments. Employers don't want to search for information. They want to be able to see all they need to know at a glance.

For those just starting their careers, resumes don't need to be more than a page. Time is valuable, and Interviewers don't want to weed through the lemonade stand you started in the sixth grade or the unpaid internship you had with you had with your uncle freshman year in high school, if you're a trade school or college graduate. I want to see real, relevant work experience from your recent training.

For a while it was a big deal to put a career goal or ambition at the top of a resume. Don't do it. It wastes precious time and space. Employers would much rather see what skills you bring to the table. This is your place to showcase the best of you. The things that don't fit in other places on your resume. This is where you can list several hard skills such as "html expertise" or "crisis mitigation." But it's also a place to list your soft skills such as "creativity" or "reliability."

If you would like more about the secret sauce of a compelling resume, read our other book in this series, "Land That Job! Resume Writing Advice from the Experts," by Becky Gosky.

Conclusion

Thank you for reading this book from cover to cover. I hope you enjoyed reading my book and have gained a lot of insights about possible job interview questions that you may encounter as you find your dream job. Please take them seriously and apply them in your everyday life so that you'll be successful.

www.ingramcontent.com/pod-product-compliance
Lightning Source LLC
Chambersburg PA
CBHW072013070526
44583CB00015B/1466